WHEN
YOU PRAY

Text copyright © Joanna Collicutt 2012
The author asserts the moral right
to be identified as the author of this work

Published by
The Bible Reading Fellowship
15 The Chambers, Vineyard
Abingdon OX14 3FE
United Kingdom
Tel: +44 (0)1865 319700
Email: enquiries@brf.org.uk
Website: www.brf.org.uk
BRF is a Registered Charity

ISBN 978 0 85746 089 9

First published 2012

10 9 8 7 6 5 4 3 2 1 0

Acknowledgments
Unless otherwise stated, scripture quotations are taken from the New Revised Standard
Version of the Bible, Anglicised edition, copyright © 1989, 1995 by the Division of Christian
Education of the National Council of the Churches of Christ in the United States of America,
and are used by permission. All rights reserved.

Scripture quotations taken from the Revised Standard Version of the Bible, copyright © 1946,
1952, 1971 by the Division of Christian Education of the National Council of the Churches of
Christ in the United States of America, are used by permission. All rights reserved.

Scripture quotations taken from the New Jerusalem Bible, published and copyright © 1985
by Darton, Longman and Todd Ltd and les Editions du Cerf, and by Doubleday, a division of
Bantam Doubleday Dell Publishing Group, Inc. Used by permission of Darton, Longman and
Todd Ltd, and Doubleday, a division of Random house, Inc.

Extracts from the Authorised Version of the Bible (The King James Bible), the rights in which
are vested in the Crown, are reproduced by permission of the Crown's Patentee, Cambridge
University Press.

Copyright material is included from *Common Worship: Services and Prayers for the Church of
England*, copyright © The Archbishops' Concil 2000. Reproduced with permission.

The paper used in the production of this publication was supplied by mills that source their
raw materials from sustainably managed forests. Soy-based inks were used in its printing and
the laminate film is biodegradable.

A catalogue record for this book is available from the British Library

Printed in Singapore by Craft Print International Ltd

WHEN YOU PRAY

Daily Bible reflections for Lent
and Easter on the Lord's Prayer

Joanna Collicutt

The BRF Lent book

For Sophie O

Contents

Introduction

'In the power of the Spirit and in union with Christ let us pray to the Father.'

The Lord's Prayer

This book is a series of Bible readings for Lent and Holy Week based on the Lord's Prayer as it is given us in Luke's Gospel. It arises from my increasing awareness in recent years that the Lord's Prayer contains all that Christians really need to know; it is the very essence of the gospel. This understanding of the Lord's Prayer is not at all new. It was the practice of the early church to prepare candidates for baptism during Lent by teaching them the Lord's Prayer and using it as the basis for instruction in the faith, sometimes supported by the creeds. In a society where most could not read or did not have access to a Bible and, before the final canon of the New Testament had even been agreed, where disputes about heresies raged, the Lord's Prayer could be held on to as the gift of Christ himself and a distillation of all that the Church understood him to be. Well into the Middle Ages, the Lord's Prayer re-mained a central framework for preaching and formed the basis of expressions of popular piety, such as mystery plays.

It was wise of those very early Christians to use a prayer rather than a set of statements to prepare people for a life of faith, for faith is not our beliefs about God; it is, rather, the relationship of trust with God that we live out. Learning how to be a Christian is not about academic study in the way we usually understand it. It is fundamentally about prayer, from which the rest of life, including study, flows. This means that, while the Lord's Prayer could be used as a kind of ancient Alpha Course manual, there is a lot more to it than that. Praying the Lord's Prayer is an expression of and vehicle for our relationship with God. It enables us to imbibe gospel values and motivates us to live them out.

Yet recently I have come to recognise that there is even more to the Lord's Prayer. This has been a gradually dawning awareness. It began with an understanding of the Christian life as one in which we not only follow *after* Jesus and not only enjoy a relationship *with* Jesus, but also are somehow incorporated *into* Jesus. A few years ago, I mentioned this in passing in a book entitled *Meeting Jesus*:

In walking the Christian way we follow [Jesus], remembering the past by walking the way of the cross (Luke 9:23) and looking ahead as we walk in newness of life. Through the Spirit, we also experience him by our side. Most mysterious of all, we find that we are walking into him... (Romans 6:3–11).[1]

This 'walking into' Jesus is a difficult idea to express. It's something about a deep belonging, a kind of identification with Jesus that goes beyond modelling our lives on his. We might want to use the term 'imitation' here. We are used to understanding this as meaning copying something or someone. However, in the Christian tradition the idea of 'imitation' has sometimes been taken further. One of the first and most delightful books I read as a young Christian was *The Imitation of Christ* (*De Imitatione Christi*), attributed to the medieval monk Thomas à Kempis. For Thomas, imitation is about following in Christ's footsteps but he also emphasises the direct relationship with Christ that his followers can experience. Thomas stretches the idea of imitation further, talking about Christ as the Way, speaking of walking the Way as a kind of 'entering into Christ' and so taking on a new identity: 'Christ [addressing The Disciple]: My son, you will be able to enter into Me so far as you are prepared to forsake yourself.'[2]

I'd known about this rather strange idea (of being 'in Christ' or 'clothed with Christ' and so on) for a long time, and it had gradually been creeping to the forefront of my mind, but I don't think I fully 'got it' until very recently— St Stephen's Day 2010, to be precise—when I was asked to read the New Testament lesson at the morning service in my local parish church. This was Luke's lengthy account of the life, witness and martyrdom of Stephen from Acts 6 and 7. It is a story that rarely gets a proper airing, among Anglicans at least, as so many of us don't go to church on Boxing Day when his feast is celebrated. I hadn't read it right through in its entirety for ages, and I was unprepared for the effect it would have on me. As I heard myself recount Stephen's assertive denunciation of the religious authorities in Jerusalem and his dying words of forgiveness, I thought, 'How like Jesus!' But then almost instantly this was replaced by another thought: 'No—Stephen is not *like* Jesus; he has kind of *become* Jesus.' As I returned to my seat, my brain began to buzz and into my head popped a familiar phrase—words spoken on the road to Damascus, shortly after Stephen's death, to a young man who had held the coats of his murderers: 'I am Jesus, whom you are persecuting.'

Finally, in my own small Damascus road moment, I started to see what Saul of Tarsus had seen.

The young Saul had looked at Stephen and had seen Jesus.

The words he heard on the Damascus road confirmed what he already knew in his heart but had been resisting at all costs in his mind: Jesus of Nazareth was alive in his followers. This was not some kind of metaphorical 'living on' but a literal reality. For the voice he heard did not say, as it so easily could have said, 'When you persecute these people it's as if you are persecuting me'; it did not say, 'When you hurt them I feel their pain, for I am in solidarity with them'; it did not say, 'I live on in these people's minds, and when you do violence to them you violate my memory'; it said, '*I am Jesus*, whom you are persecuting.' Saul took this statement at face value; Jesus and his followers were one. The rest of Paul's life can be understood as a response to this literal understanding.

I too have come to an understanding, helped greatly by Paul, and it is centred on the Lord's Prayer. It is simply this: in praying the Lord's Prayer, human beings take on the character of Christ. We don't just act in obedience to Christ or in conformity with Christ, although, of course, we do both of these. In some very deep sense, we are incorporated into Christ and are 'in union' with Christ. In this series of biblical reflections we shall explore this mystery further. Lent is, after all, the period in which Christians have traditionally sought to identify more deeply with Christ.

As Paul discovered, this is a transforming work of the Spirit, but it is also a work that is wrought through the medium of words. The words are very important, and the most important of them is *Abba*, for through the work of Christ human beings are offered the possibility of an intimate parent–child relationship with the divine. Here, at the outset, we find a trinitarian framework: we pray in union with Christ through the power of the Spirit, and our prayer is directed to the Father. Thus we are caught up into the Godhead.

The very special significance of the words of the Lord's Prayer is something that has been held on to over many generations and, from time to time, has become distorted and debased. Bitter—indeed, violent—conflicts have raged over the translation of the prayer. At times its words have been treated as a magic formula. There have existed subcultures in which ten Paternosters have been thought to do ten times as much good as one. I have even had something of this attitude myself.

When I was a child of about seven, my Sunday school class was given an assignment to learn the Lord's Prayer. The next week, when my turn came to recite it, I promptly went ahead at breakneck speed. 'You don't get a prize for getting to the end first,' the teacher remarked. 'Have you any idea what it means?' I did express my vague thought that 'temptation' was what I had felt when my mother left a freshly iced coffee-walnut cake unattended on the kitchen table, but I couldn't get much further than that. The teacher wasn't best pleased. Nevertheless, I felt aggrieved rather than abashed: I had quite a sense of achievement at being able to get my tongue around those archaic words, and I thought she was expecting too much in requiring that I understand them as well.

With the hindsight of many years, and perhaps oddly in view of the high premium that academics like me place on understanding, I think my childhood self had a point. For Jesus does not ask his followers to understand this prayer; he asks them to pray it. The legendary words of the medieval Dominican Father, John of Saxony, are illuminating here:

A layman once put this question to him: 'Master, is the *Our Father* worth as much in the mouths of simple folk like myself, who do not know its full meaning, as in the mouths of learned clerks who understand all that they are saying?' To this he answered: 'Of a surety it is; just as a precious stone is equally valuable in the hands of one who does not know its full worth as it would be even if he did.'[3]

My prayer for those who read this book is that you will have a sense of the great privilege that has been granted to us of holding a precious gem in our hands, of being able to delight in its radiance, play with its many facets, plumb its depths, gain a sense of peace and security from its touch, and in so doing deepen our awareness of our union with Christ.

Luke's version

There are two versions of the Lord's Prayer in the New Testament: Matthew 6:9–15 and Luke 11:2–4. It seems that Matthew's version established itself as the prayer of the church from earliest times. The second-century Christian document known as the *Didache* contains a version which quite closely resembles Matthew's but adds, 'For yours is the power and the glory' (the doxology). A doxology similar to this is to be found in some third- and fourth-century manuscripts of Matthew's Gospel. Perhaps it was inadvertently added by copyists who had become used to praying the doxology in their daily devotions. At any rate, this meant that Matthew's version plus the doxology 'For Thine is the kingdom, the power and the glory, for ever and ever' found its way via the Latin Bible into the English Prayer Book of 1549, based on translations by William Tyndale and Myles Coverdale. This form of the Lord's Prayer became deeply ingrained in the consciousness of the English-speaking world until the rise of secularism towards the end of the 20th century, and is still known and cherished by millions.

Luke's version, on the other hand, has been rather neglected in the prayer of the church, and this is one reason that I have chosen to use it as the basis of these Lenten devotions. We are less familiar with it and so may come to it afresh. In general, where there are two versions of material, Matthew's tends to be more elaborate and 'poetic', and Luke's more elegant and 'edgy', as in the Beatitudes (Matthew 5:3–11; Luke 6:20–23). While it's possible that Matthew knew Luke's version of the prayer and elaborated it, or that Luke knew Matthew's version and condensed it, it seems most likely that Matthew and Luke simply had access to different Christian communities with different recollections of the precise words of Jesus. Indeed, we shall see that there are traces of the Lord's Prayer in the Gospels of Mark and John too. The gist is the same, even though the wording differs. There are also, of course, different wordings of Luke 11:2–4 in the various English Bible translations. I have used the New Jerusalem Bible translation, as this is the most accurate in terms of both language and theology.[4]

In addition to its relative neglect, I have another reason for using Luke's version of the Lord's Prayer: Luke is the author of Acts. It was, after all, Luke's wonderful accounts of the death of Stephen and Saul's encounter with Jesus on the road to Damascus that first drew my attention to the way that the faithful Christian comes not only to resemble Christ but to identify with Christ. I have a deep respect for Luke.

Finally, and perhaps most importantly of all, Luke's version of the Lord's Prayer begins simply with one word: 'Father'. If we are to pray 'by, with and in Christ',[5] that is where we must begin.

Ash Wednesday to Saturday
WHEN YOU PRAY

The first Christians were praying the Lord's Prayer long before Matthew and Luke committed it to writing in their Gospels. Matthew and Luke each recorded the version used by his own community, and they both took care to place it in the context of Jesus' wider teaching on prayer. The Lord gave us a special form of words, but these words sum up an attitude of prayer.

Matthew places the prayer in the middle of the Sermon on the Mount, as part of an extended piece of teaching on how to live as a disciple of Jesus. Luke places it later in his story, at the beginning of a section devoted exclusively to the nature of prayer and directly after the parable of the good Samaritan and the account of Jesus' visit to Martha's home. It's not often noticed, but the Samaritan and Mary, Martha's sister, have a lot in common and can perhaps be treated as a pair. Both have a correctly attentive attitude and both are held up as models of Christian discipleship. Both are contrasted with other, no doubt holy, people who are preoccupied with their religious obligations in the public or domestic sphere. The Samaritan is not distracted by the legal demands of the temple cult, and he can thus see and draw near to the man who is so desperately in need of help (Luke 10:33). Likewise, Mary is not distracted by the duties expected of her as host or deacon, and she can thus listen at the feet of Jesus (v. 39).

Prayer requires us to be attentive, and to turn our attention in the right direction. This attitude of attentiveness may be a contemplation of the person of Christ; it may be a noticing of the needs of others in the world and his church; it may, like the prodigal son's (15:17), be an insight into our own deep need of God and a turning towards him. What it won't be is ruminative worry or mental attempts to solve problems. Worry and problem-solving, focusing on the job in hand, do have their place in this life, but they are not part of the prayerful attitude, which, as Jesus says to Martha, is fundamentally 'better' (10:42).

To cultivate this kind of prayerful attitude is to be obedient to Jesus, but it is also to identify with Jesus. Praying 'in the name of Jesus' means to pray 'in accordance with his nature', and this is the essence of the Christian life: 'whatever you do, in word or deed, do everything in the name of the Lord Jesus' (Colossians 3:17). We often end our prayers with phrases such as 'In thy name we pray' or 'in the name of Jesus Christ', and it can be rather like a kind of signal that the prayer is coming to an end (as, for some years, our children thought grace before meals was a way of saying, 'Ready, steady, eat!'). But we need to remember that acting, thinking or praying in the name of someone is far more than this. When we pray in Christ's name, we are placing ourselves under his authority and protection and taking up an intentional stance that is in accordance with his nature. So, for instance, it would be self-contradictory to pray for harm to come to our enemies in the name of Jesus; in fact, to do so would be taking his name in vain. That's what Jesus means when he talks about people who do great deeds 'in my name' but whom he never knew (Matthew 7:22–23). He is drawing a distinction between 'name' and 'identity'. Such people use Jesus' name but they have not identified with his nature. As he says at length in John 10, Jesus knows the identity of his sheep because they conform to his nature, and so they can be easily recognised. Apart from this, the issue of outward names is irrelevant.

Whether we ask in Jesus' name, gather in his name, welcome strangers in his name or are hated because of his name, it is in accordance with his nature, just as he acted in accordance with the Father (John 10:25), and the Spirit acts in accordance with him (14:26).

So, before we begin our study of the Lord's Prayer itself, we will prepare ourselves by paying attention to Jesus' attitude to prayer as it is told us by the Gospel writers.

Teach us to pray

He was praying in a certain place, and after he had finished, one of his disciples said to him, 'Lord, teach us to pray, as John taught his disciples.'
LUKE 11:1

Was Jesus of Nazareth a religious man? I think many of us would be inclined to answer 'no' to this question. He certainly appears to have been critical of several aspects of the religion of his day, sitting rather lightly to its purity demands, and he came into marked conflict with the religious authorities. It was, after all, an incident in the courts of the temple that led to his arrest, trial and conviction for blasphemy. He seems to have had little patience with outward religious forms that did not express inner spiritual realities.

Is it, perhaps, better to describe him as a spiritual man or a holy man? If we look more closely at his way of life, we find that here too he seems to subvert what we usually think of as the spiritual or holy. Our ideas of spirituality have become very much bound up with silence and stillness, 'being rather than doing', asceticism, withdrawal from the corrupting influences of the world (Thomas à Kempis was strong on this), sacred space and ritual and, above all, a regular discipline of prayer that supports a rule of life.

It is, then, quite surprising that not until we are eleven chapters into Luke's Gospel do we find any real discussion of prayer. Luke presents us instead with a man who bursts on to the scene in Galilee with an assertion that 'the Spirit of the Lord is upon me' and a proclamation that the year of the Lord's favour has arrived (4:18–19). It is a time marked by healing and social justice, and, indeed, Jesus moves on from this proclamation to carry out a whole series of healing and liberating acts. If you were to try to answer the question of what sort of man Jesus of Nazareth was, on the basis of Luke 4—11, you would have to say that he was a highly charismatic, somewhat controversial figure who gathered a group of followers and went around speaking at local community centres, proclaiming a vision of social justice and making it real in the lives of ordinary folk. He comes over as an activist, perhaps even a political activist, and he likens himself to a physician—someone who goes about fixing broken people (Matthew 9:12; Mark 2:17; Luke 5:31).

If you want a model of a holy man, it is to be found not in Jesus but in John the Baptist. John lives in the desert, away from the fleshpots of the town; he and his band of male disciples follow a strict regime of prayer and fasting, and he has his own distinctive sacred ritual—baptism for the repentance of sins.

Jesus, on the other hand, doesn't fast, nor does he require fasting of his disciples. In fact, when they are hungry he is quite willing to flout the sabbath laws to satisfy their wants, and he regularly breaks the sabbath in order to pursue his agenda of healing and liberation. Furthermore, Jesus does not obviously engage in ritual and he inhabits profane, not sacred space. He journeys to centres of population rather than permanently inhabiting the wilderness and calling people to him. He touches people who suffer from health conditions that have the power to pollute those with whom they come into contact; he keeps company with folk whose morals are at best questionable and at worst utterly unacceptable; and he counts women among his close friends and followers. To cap it all, he attends rather a lot of parties, where the food is plentiful and the wine flows freely. In this spirit, when Jesus sends out 70 disciples (Luke 10), he gives them instructions to journey to centres of population to proclaim, to heal and, of course, to eat—but nothing is said about prayer.

None of this sits quite right with conventional ideas of a holy man pursuing a spiritual agenda. The scribes and Pharisees are constantly pointing this out. Rather more surprisingly, John the Baptist, who had expected such great things from Jesus at the time of his baptism, seems to have had his doubts too, for he sends messengers to ask Jesus, 'Are you the one who is to come, or are we to wait for another?' (Matthew 11:3; Luke 7:19). Jesus' answer is illuminating. He doesn't point to his personal spirituality or holiness of life. Instead he gives a pragmatic response, rather like a doctor reporting the outcome data from a trial of a new medicine: 'Look what is happening to people—you do the maths!'

Now, this is all very well, but if you were a follower of Jesus it may not be quite what you were expecting, especially if you had previously been a follower of John, as was probably the case for some of Jesus' disciples. A regular conventional pattern of religious devotion would be rather helpful. In a world that is populated by signs and wonders, where everything seems to be changing, where the holy man behaves in unconventional ways, piety can provide a sense of security. Perhaps this lies behind the request, 'Lord, teach us to pray, as John taught his disciples.'

Notice, though, that this request doesn't come out of the blue. Luke tells us that the disciple who makes it has observed Jesus at prayer and has seized the moment. There are, in fact, several references to Jesus praying, made almost in passing, in earlier chapters of Luke's Gospel (6:12; 9:18, 28), and from this we see that prayer was habitual for him.

This is perhaps the most distinctive characteristic of Jesus of Nazareth. Because, for him, the difference between sacred and profane is blurred, his prayer is not an act of piety but the essential heartbeat of his whole life. All his activism is powered by prayer, and, like the beating heart or the breath of life, that prayer is so fundamental and so pervasive that it seems to require little in the way of self-conscious reflection. The fact that prayer is hardly mentioned before this disciple raises the issue is a measure not of its absence from the life of Jesus but of how much it is taken for granted as the basis of his life. When he sends out the 70, to mention prayer would be like saying, 'Don't forget to breathe!' Jesus is so in touch with his Father, and the relationship of prayer is so natural for him (we see this from his joyful and intimate outpouring to God in the previous chapter: 10:21), that to instruct people in 'how to do it' may seem somewhat contrived. Yet when asked to do so, Jesus graciously accedes. People can, after all, benefit greatly from training in good breathing techniques.

Prayer

God, in whom we live and move and have our being, teach me to breathe deeply of your Spirit. In Jesus' name I pray.

Thursday

Too many words

'When you are praying, do not heap up empty phrases as the Gentiles do; for they think that they will be heard because of their many words. Do not be like them, for your Father knows what you need before you ask him.'

MATTHEW 6:7–8

These words of Jesus give us a clue as to why his disciples might have felt the need to ask him about techniques of prayer. He seems to have been, in prayer at least, a man of few words. But in fact, as the reference to 'the Gentiles' indicates, this was the character of much Jewish prayer. It does not waste words.

The people of Israel saw prayer as something of a paradox: the expression of an intimate personal relationship with the all-powerful LORD who created the cosmos. This relationship was possible because of the covenant that the LORD had made and remade with his people (Genesis 9 and 17; Joshua 24; 2 Samuel 23:5; Psalm 89). The covenant required them to meditate on the law—the Torah—to live it out and, above all, to be utterly centred on God. Doing all of this was not a way to 'keep God sweet' but an expression of the privileged relationship that his people had with him. The covenant was initiated by God in his grace and, in his grace, he asked his chosen people to, as it were, rise to the occasion and respond in kind.

At the time of Jesus it is likely that faithful Jews recited the Shema (Deuteronomy 6:4, possibly continuing up to verse

9) morning and evening, as well as prayers of blessing at various points throughout the day. The Shema is economical of words and is, in some respects, like the Lord's Prayer. It sums up all one needs to know about God: God is one, we are his, and we are to respond to him with wholehearted love. There is, however, an obvious difference. The Shema is an assertion about the nature of God and our relationship with him. It is thus somewhere between what we understand as a prayer and what we might call a creed. The Lord's Prayer, on the other hand, doesn't assert truths about God; it addresses God directly and intimately, and in this sense it is more like a psalm (for example, Psalm 8 or 139).

Despite the fact that Jesus appears to have sat lightly to the purity requirements of the Jewish law, it is almost certain that he would have engaged in the obligatory daily prayers, including the recital of the Shema, as would John the Baptist. But it seems that a holy man with a following would have been expected to have his own additional pattern of devotion that he would teach his disciples. One reason for this is that there was a strong expectation that the current epoch was passing away, and new prayers were needed for the new age that was about to dawn.

Yet, as we have seen, Jesus seems to have been a bit reticent with regard to formal prayer, and in this extract from Matthew's Gospel he begins his teaching by stressing the need to avoid praying with too many words. The reason given is that wordy prayers are the mark of people who do not stand in a covenant relationship with God, who therefore try to use their prayers as a way of grabbing God's attention and then, when they have got it, getting him to dance to their tune. The expression 'heap up empty phrases' is a translation of a single Greek word, *battalogēsēte*. It has quite a specific meaning that relates to babbling magical incantations, something that would have been anathema to pious Jews at the time of Jesus. This sort of prayer is a kind of idolatry, for it focuses on the words as instruments of control and treats God as an object that can be controlled by them. How different from the Shema!

Jesus' disciples were Jews, for the most part pious, and certainly not Gentiles. So why did they need to beware of many words? The answer seems to be that they were human beings, and human beings have a propensity to get seduced by language and then entangled in it. Although the aspiration of Jewish prayer is true and noble, and radically different from the prayer of cultures that seemed intent on making God jump through hoops, it is possible that at the time of Jesus it had become corrupted. For the best part of a millennium, the Jewish nation had suffered at the hands of foreign invaders, captors and occupiers—just the sort of people who prayed by 'piling up empty phrases'. The covenant relationship with God, which had felt so secure in the time of Abraham, Moses and David, had more recently gone through periods when it seemed to be hanging by a thread. Under these conditions it is all too easy for faith to turn from the expression of a secure and cooperative relationship into something else—a desperate attempt to keep that relationship on the road—and with more desperation come more words.

So, notice how Jesus puts the brakes on this desperation by reminding us that God is our Father—an assurance of a relationship rather than an abstract statement about the nature of God. It is because God loves us that he knows what we need, not because he is an impersonal omniscient being. If we could only relax into the fact that God's relationship with us is absolutely secure, we would find that we don't need so many words.

Words can let people down. It isn't possible to build a stairway to heaven (a tower of Babel?) with words. Too many words can mean that we can't hear ourselves think and, more importantly, we can't be attentive to the still small divine voice. Too many words are not only pointless, not only idolatrous, not only a mark of anxiety, but they are also counterproductive. They can build a barrier between human beings and the life of the Spirit, a barrier that we can sometimes purposefully shore up in order to keep God at arm's length.

A couple of years ago, I attended a conference for Christian survivors of serious conditions affecting the brain. The delegates were discussing their experience of church worship. The phrase 'too many words' soon emerged and summed up well the thrust of their discussion, and it was with their witness in mind that I chose the title for today's reading. These people felt bombarded by words in church—overwhelmed, confused, stressed and exhausted. What they said was prophetic, for all of us have experienced something like this in church, though we rarely name it, and, if we are not careful, we can carry the 'too many words' of public worship into our personal prayer life.

When we pray, we are not telling or even asking God to do things; we are participating in a love relationship, and you don't need many words for that.

Prayer
Speak, Lord, for your servant is listening.

Friday

Up the mountain

And after he had dismissed the crowds, he went up the mountain by himself to pray. When evening came, he was there alone.
Matthew 14:23

After saying farewell to them, he went up on the mountain to pray.
Mark 6:46

Now during those days he went out to the mountain to pray; and he spent the night in prayer to God.
Luke 6:12

Now about eight days after these sayings Jesus took with him Peter and John and James, and went up on the mountain to pray.
Luke 9:28

Mountains play a very special part in the culture of the people who live around them. They inspire awe and wonder because of their immense scale, the changes to their appearance that come with different weather conditions, the challenge and danger they offer to those who would climb them, and the views that can be achieved at their heights. Mountains are always treated with respect and are often seen as sacred—places of encounter with the holy or transcendent.

The ancient people of Israel were no exception here. Noah and his family found a place of safety on Mount Ararat, Abraham's journeying involved several sacred mountain places, Moses encountered God in the burning bush on Mount

Horeb and later received the law on Mount Sinai, and the holy city of Jerusalem was built on a hill.

The holiness of mountains follows naturally from Hebrew cosmology. God inhabited 'the heavens', which, according to Genesis 1, are located beyond the sky that we can see with its sun, moon and stars. So if you want to get close to God, you have to go up. There were tales of people being able to fly heavenwards—prophets such as Elijah and Ezekiel in their heavenly chariots—but for most people the nearest one could get to God would be to climb a mountain.

The idea that God is literally 'up there' may seem primitive to us, in the light of all that we now know about the earth orbiting our sun in one of millions of galaxies. Yet most of us continue to think of good and heavenly things being upwards, and base and miserable things being downwards. Psychologists describe positive, optimistic mood as 'elevated' and negative, pessimistic mood as 'depressed'. We talk of 'rising to an occasion' or 'sinking so low', 'reaching for the stars' or 'hitting rock bottom', 'growing up' and 'dumbing down'. All our human hierarchies place the most important person at the top and the least important at the bottom. Yesterday we reflected on the very human mistake of trying to build a stairway to heaven by piling words up on top of each other. The sense that what is good and true and powerful is 'up there' goes very deep in us.

Perhaps it has its beginnings in our early childhood when we raise our arms, longing to be lifted high up into the warmth, love and safety of our parents' embrace. When our daughter was very small, she had a habit of raising up her arms and saying, 'Mummy—I love you up to the ceiling, up to the sky!' This posture—standing with arms reaching up and eyes looking skyward—has been traditional in formal

Jewish and then Christian prayer for thousands of years. At the beginning of the great prayer of thanksgiving spoken over the Communion bread and wine, the minister says something known in Latin as the *sursum corda*, which in translation means simply, 'Up with your hearts!' Then the people respond by saying that they are doing just that—lifting them heavenwards to the Lord. It's as if the gathered assembly is saying to God, 'We love you up to the ceiling, up to the sky!'

Jesus also seems to have had the instinct that getting nearer his beloved Father would involve upward movement. Matthew, Mark and Luke all tell us that Jesus looked up to heaven before he blessed the bread and fish when he fed the 5000 (Matthew 14:19; Mark 6:41; Luke 9:16), and John tells us that Jesus did this on the night he was betrayed, when he began his very long prayer of thanksgiving, sometimes referred to as his 'high priestly prayer' (John 17:1). But Jesus also climbed mountains, sometimes alone, sometimes with his disciples, and it seems that it was on mountains that he felt closest to God.

Climbing a mountain is a bit like going into the desert. The clamour of the world fades away and all is quiet. Getting there is strenuous and the terrain can be inhospitable. Nature is close at hand, vivid and immense in scale, and we can feel very small. Defences are stripped away and we must face ourselves as we really are. The physical exertion involved leaves little room for chatter. As words are laid aside, a space is cleared to hear and welcome the still small divine voice.

Yet mountain travel is also different from travel in desert or plain. All travel involves a changing vista, but when we climb a mountain it is possible to keep the route we have travelled in view. 'Gosh!' we pant. 'Look how far we have come!' We may also see the place where we started our journey: 'Look at the houses and cars—they look like toys! And the people look like tiny insects!' We continue to see the same vista but its scale has changed. Those things that loomed so large now don't seem very big at all. We gain a different perspective, perhaps even a heavenly perspective.

Going up is absolutely central to Jesus' identity. He looked and climbed up to pray, in order to hold on to that heavenly perspective, without which he could not act aright. He was raised up on the cross. He rose up from the dead. Finally, he said farewell to his disciples on a mountain and departed from them upwards (Matthew 28:16; Acts 1:9–12). This should not surprise us, because the work of Jesus is to raise up men and women with him—to raise us from lethargy to action, to raise our mood and our spirits, to raise us to our full humanity, to raise our moral status and to raise us from death to life, to pull us up with him into the intimate embrace of the Father. The typical dynamic of Jesus is upwards and onwards.

Prayer requires us to be attentive and to turn our attention in the right direction. If we are to be like our Master, we must lay aside too many words, be prepared to turn our attention upwards and seek a heavenly perspective.

Prayer

Lord, help me to grasp that I have been raised with Christ and my life is hidden deep in Christ. So, may I set my mind on things that are above.

In your room

But he would withdraw to deserted places and pray.
Luke 5:16

'And whenever you pray, do not be like the hypocrites; for they love to stand and pray in the synagogues and at the street corners, so that they may be seen by others. Truly I tell you, they have received their reward. But whenever you pray, go into your room and shut the door and pray to your Father who is in secret; and your Father who sees in secret will reward you.'
Matthew 6:5–6

It's all very well to talk about a 'heavenly perspective', but what might this actually mean? After all, many of us are familiar with the phrase 'so heavenly-minded as to be no earthly use', which seems to regard 'heavenly-minded' as being equivalent to 'away with the fairies'. Here, a heavenly-minded person is seen as a kind of daydreamer who is incapable of effective action in the real world.

But Jesus is not like this. As we have seen, in his life, prayer and action were intimately linked with each other, not set against each other. He was able to act effectively in the real world precisely because his heavenly perspective was maintained through his life of prayer. However, Jesus also repeatedly asserted that there is a kind of human 'worldly perspective' which is deeply at odds with the things of God.

This worldly perspective is essentially about seeing God as an object who might be flattered or manipulated, having personal advancement as our highest priority, paying more attention to outward appearance than inward realities, and desiring power over others and adulation from them. It is this worldly perspective that is presented by Satan to Jesus during his time of testing in the wilderness. Satan suggests that Jesus use his special abilities to advance his own agenda, test God out, and dominate and subdue the empires of the world. This temptation is replayed later at Caesarea Philippi, when Jesus says to Peter, 'Get behind me, Satan!' (Matthew 16:23; Mark 8:33), so it is worth reflecting a bit on what provokes Jesus to utter these apparently harsh words to one of his most devoted followers.

Matthew's version is most instructive here (Matthew 16:13–28). He tells how Peter correctly identifies Jesus as 'the Messiah, the Son of the living God', to which Jesus joyfully responds, 'Flesh and blood has not revealed this to you, but my Father in heaven.' Jesus is saying that Peter has been appropriately attentive and has thus attained a heavenly perspective: he has seen that Jesus is God's anointed one. But very quickly Peter loses this perspective and urges Jesus to reject the way of the cross; so it is evident to Jesus that he is setting his mind 'not on divine things but on human things'. Jesus goes on to make the deeply challenging statement that the way of the cross is the only way both for the Messiah and for his followers.

A similar incident is recounted in John's Gospel, and it explains Jesus' apparent need to get away from people by withdrawing to deserted, often mountainous, places to pray. After his account of the feeding of the 5000, John tells us, 'When Jesus realised that they were about to come and take him by force to make him king, he withdrew again to the mountain by himself' (6:15). The crowds were so impressed by the signs and wonders that Jesus was working that they naturally wanted to hail him as their political leader and confer on him all the trappings of power. If Peter was a stumbling-block at Caesarea Philippi, these crowds were a potential millstone. Jesus had to turn away from Peter and he had to get away from the crowds. It's as if the worldly perspective that feeds on self-advancement, adulation and power, the perspective that offers the wide and easy road, might have dragged him down if he had not taken decisive action and distanced himself from it.

Jesus also says to his followers, if this is a problem for me, you can be sure it will be a problem for you too. People may not want to make you king, but there are other pitfalls out there: 'Woe to you when all speak well of you' (Luke 6:26a). It is so easy to 'do religion' for the wrong reasons. This is true for all Christians but, speaking as a member of the clergy, I can attest to the fact that it is a particular challenge to those of us in church leadership positions. It is so affirming when members of our congregations praise our teaching, our pastoral care or the spiritual guidance we have given. There is nothing wrong in this: we all thrive on praise and it is good to receive it and to give it. But there is a danger, to which we need to be ever attentive: we can begin to enjoy the praise so much that we start to see our religious activities as ways of getting affirmation—as means to an end.

When Jesus talks about the 'hypocrites' who pray in a very obvious way in public, he is drawing our attention to this issue. Even prayer, the most apparently heavenly directed activity of all, can be hijacked by a worldly perspective. This is a danger that needs to be managed, and it is best managed by 'getting away'. If you can't jump in a boat and cross a lake or climb a mountain or go into the wilderness, at least you should be able to find a secret place where you live and work. In a society where people did not have individual domestic spaces to call their own, the 'room' that Jesus speaks of refers to a storeroom or barn. Our equivalent might be the loft or garage, even a cupboard under the stairs. In spaces such as these, free from the distractions of too many words, free from an appreciative audience for our public persona and free from persuasive voices that speak to us of self-interest and personal advancement, we have a hope of gaining a heavenly perspective and connecting with our Father—and it is with 'Father' that the Lord's Prayer begins.

Prayer

Lord, let me love you for yourself and as myself.

Week 1

FATHER

Now, after a period of preparation, we come to the Lord's Prayer itself, by which I mean the words of the Lord's Prayer. We have heard Jesus' teaching that too many words—sounding a cacophony, invoked magically, intoned meaninglessly—can form a barrier between God and the human heart. But words are not in themselves bad: John's Gospel describes Jesus as the *logos*, the eternal Word, God's speech-act of communication with human beings (1:1). Words are important, and, in Luke's spare version of the Lord's Prayer, not a word is wasted.

Like the rest of the New Testament, Luke's Gospel is written in Greek. Jesus may well have known Greek but it is certain that he usually spoke a Semitic language, probably Aramaic or possibly Hebrew. So, the prayer that has come down to us in English is a translation of a translation of a memory of the prayer that Jesus taught. It is likely that Jesus taught his disciples about prayer on more than one occasion, and he himself may have used slightly different versions. So, while we can be sure that the gist of the prayer is as Jesus gave it (Matthew and Luke's versions are not too different), we don't have a verbatim record of Jesus' 'original' words.

We can be sure of one word, though. Everybody is agreed that the prayer must have begun with the Semitic word *Abba*.[6] This word is mentioned in its original form in three places in the Greek New Testament, always associated with the prayer of Jesus, and we will be looking at each of them this week. It is clear that, from the earliest days of the church, the word *Abba* resounded in people's memories in a way that immediately brought Jesus of Nazareth to mind. It seems to have been somewhat like a catchphrase that could be used to identify him. Just as his habitual act of breaking bread opened the eyes of the two disciples on the road to Emmaus to the identity of their travelling companion, the blessing he spoke—which surely began with *Abba*—would have opened their ears (Luke 24:30).

This word is given a significant place at the beginning of the Lord's Prayer. Scholars who have attempted to reconstruct the prayer as an original spoken Aramaic poem have suggested that the opening *Abba* would be followed by a breath or a pause before continuing with the rhythmic petitions that follow. This word is not to be rushed. But when Jesus said '*Abba*', what did he mean?

The word *Abba* originated in the Aramaic language but, by the time of Jesus, it had become incorporated into everyday Hebrew speech as well. It refers to a biological father or an old respected man. It was used in the extended family circle rather than the wider public sphere of religion or business. It is an easy word for a small child to utter but it is not a diminutive version of an adult form; the same word would have been used by both children and adults. It is at once intimate and respectful. Perhaps the nearest we have come to it in modern times would be the Victorian 'Papa'. In present-day English, the best (or least unsatisfactory) translation is 'Father'.

The precise meaning of *Abba* in any given context is not always clear, however. This is because Aramaic is an ambiguous language: *Abba* could mean 'my father', 'your father', 'the father' or 'our father' (hence the 'Our Father' of Matthew's version of the Lord's Prayer). *Abba* could also be used for talking about father or talking to him. This uncertainty can be annoying for scholars and translators but it does allow things to be left open in ways that can turn out to be creative and helpful.

Luke's simple 'Father' keeps the open, ambiguous sense of the Aramaic. It allows for the fact that Jesus' relationship to this father may not be exactly the same as ours. It leaves open the possibility that this father is not just the Father of the Hebrew people, not just the Father of the Christians, but the Father of all humankind. It also captures the way in which *Abba* is probably used here both as a direct form of address and as an assertion about a relationship (something like 'You are Father!').

This brings us to the most important question of all: who is this *Abba*? This is where Jesus' use of *Abba* is so significant and distinctive, if not completely unique, for Jesus seems to have used *Abba* habitually as a form of direct address to the LORD God.

In the Old Testament, most of which is written in Hebrew, God is never addressed as 'Father'. By the time of Jesus, prayers in the Hebrew language beginning 'Our Father' (*'ābînû*) or 'My Father' (*'ābî*) were being used at least occasionally as part of formal Jewish worship. What seems to have been different about Jesus is that instead of using formal liturgical language to express the fatherhood of God, he used a word from everyday family life. (I get a powerful sense of what this might have felt like when, from time to time, I give consecrated bread to someone at the Communion rail and he responds to my words 'The body of Christ' with a natural 'Thank you' rather than the more formal and churchy 'Amen'.)

Here again we see in Jesus a breakdown of the divide between the sacred and profane, between the extraordinary and ordinary, and an awareness of the divine presence in all parts of life, not just public religion. His use of respectful but definitely domestic language to refer to the Creator of the cosmos also signifies an unprecedented and extraordinary degree of intimacy. It is a degree of intimacy which would be beyond human beings, were it not for Jesus—for, as we saw in last Friday's reflection, the work of Jesus is to pull us up into an intimate relationship with his Father, with 'my Father and your Father... my God and your God' (John 20:17b). Christians claim this reality—the possibility of an intimate relationship with God—by joining with their Master in addressing God as *Abba*, or Papa. At the deepest level, to be able and willing to begin our prayers with *Abba* is a mark of Christ.

In the garden

They went to a place called Gethsemane; and he said to his disciples, 'Sit here while I pray.' ... He said, 'Abba, Father, for you all things are possible; remove this cup from me; yet, not what I want, but what you want.'
MARK 14:32, 36

'You are my Son, the Beloved; with you I am well pleased.'
MARK 1:11B; LUKE 3:22B

We are used to the idea that there are two versions of the Lord's Prayer in the New Testament—Matthew's and Luke's. In fact, this prayer can be found in more subtle guise in the other two Gospels as well. The Gospel of Mark was almost certainly the first to be written (about 35 years after the death of Jesus), and it is in Mark's account of Jesus' prayer in Gethsemane that we have the earliest written record of something like the Lord's Prayer: Jesus begins his prayer, '*Abba*', goes on to ask to be spared from his coming time of testing or trial, and then asks for God's will to be done.

Here in his hour of greatest need, Jesus turns to his Father. At times of crisis we turn to, even call out for, one who has loved and taken care of us from childhood. This is most often our mother (there are frequent and poignant reports of soldiers dying on the battlefield calling for their mothers), but sometimes it is our father, a grandparent or a sibling. The special relationship that we have with our primary caregivers is described as an 'attachment bond' by psychologists, and the small child's determination to stick close to this figure is called 'attachment behaviour'. It begins in infancy, is at its most marked in early childhood and is reworked when we fall in love. Then it seems almost to disappear—that is, until we run into trouble, when it re-emerges as a need to be close to those with whom we have formed an attachment bond.

Within a secure attachment relationship, we treat our beloved caregiver both as a 'safe haven'—someone to whom we can run and hide when things get tough—and a 'secure base' whose presence gives us the confidence to venture forward into the world.

Jesus clearly had this sort of deep and secure bond with the one he addressed as *Abba*. While his relationship with his mother must have been vitally important to him as a young child, his relationship with a father-figure would have been more ambiguous. Jesus did not know his biological father and was an adopted member of Joseph's family. Luke recounts an incident in which, in response to Mary's description of Joseph as 'your father', Jesus emphatically states that *God* is his Father (Luke 2:48–49). Perhaps Jesus always felt on the edge of his family circle, as if he didn't quite fit. Perhaps there was yearning for family intimacy of a different kind.

As we grow up, we face certain big questions about ourselves and the universe. The two most pressing of these are 'Who am I?' and 'Am I worth anything?' We need to work out the answers to such questions within a relationship of love. If we feel truly loved, we can become ourselves, know ourselves and be secure that we are worthy of love. Jesus too must have struggled with these human questions of identity and worth, but, we are told, when he was baptised by John he had a dramatic experience that answered such questions once and for all.

Jesus comes *up* out of the water and gains a literally heavenly perspective as the skies are opened and a voice from beyond speaks directly to him. The message is short and sweet. First, Jesus is assured that he is the Son of God. Second, he is assured that the relationship with God is a love relationship. Having been made secure in this relationship, Jesus is only then told that he is also personally worthy— pleasing to God.

The Gospel writers use the literary conventions of their time to depict deep and complex truths. Perhaps Jesus' assurance of his Father's love didn't come in an instant with physically parted skies, but come it did. His subsequent life and ministry are full of it, and his talk constantly returns to his bond with this Father who is beyond the skies in heaven.

The possibility of addressing God as Father is considered in just one place in the Old Testament, and it is linked with the image of a rock. As part of his covenant, God promises David that he will one day be able to address him in this way: 'He shall cry to me, "You are my Father, my God, and the Rock of my salvation!"' (Psalm 89:26). Jesus gains a sense of security from his attachment bond to his Father, who functions for him not only as his safe haven, a 'Rock of Ages', but also as his secure base—a rock-solid foundation whose presence gives him the courage to venture forth and face trials, and on which everything else in his life is built.

Some of us, who have been fortunate enough to experience a father who has acted as our rock, will identify strongly with Jesus' use of paternal language and images to express his secure and loving relationship with God. An increasing number of us will find talk of God as 'Father' difficult to relate to, or downright offputting. Present-day Western society is not strongly patriarchal; families are often without a father; sadly, some people's experience of their father has been of an unreliable or abusive figure. It is important, then, to remember that Jesus' own family life was not straightforward. He was, after all, conceived out of wedlock, brought up in the household of his stepfather (who probably died when Jesus was in his teens) and living alongside half- or stepbrothers and stepsisters. Somehow, in the midst of all this, his astonishing relationship with God emerged and then flourished. He wants this for us too—an intimate, mutually respectful relationship with God, in which we feel loved, secure and worthy, and from which we can go forth to do great things. This is what Jesus means by *Abba*: not someone who is essentially masculine, not even someone who is essentially parental, but someone who cares for us and delights in us, with a love-bond stronger than death.

Prayer

Abba, caregiver, be to me a safe haven and secure base.

Monday

Another garden

And the LORD God planted a garden in Eden, in the east; and there he put the man whom he had formed... They heard the sound of the LORD God walking in the garden at the time of the evening breeze, and the man and his wife hid themselves from the presence of the LORD God among the trees of the garden. But the LORD God called to the man, and said to him, 'Where are you?' He said, 'I heard the sound of you in the garden, and I was afraid, because I was naked; and I hid myself.' He said, 'Who told you that you were naked? Have you eaten from the tree of which I commanded you not to eat?' The man said, 'The woman whom you gave to be with me, she gave me fruit from the tree, and I ate.' Then the LORD God said to the woman, 'What is this that you have done?' The woman said, 'The serpent tricked me, and I ate.' ... He drove out the man; and at the east of the garden of Eden he placed the cherubim, and a sword flaming and turning to guard the way to the tree of life.

Genesis 2:8; 3:8–13, 24

When Jesus cries '*Abba*' in the garden, he is at a crossroads: before him open the wide and easy way of retreating to the Judean hills, and perhaps regrouping his followers to stir up a violent uprising, and the alternative hard and narrow way of staying put and awaiting arrest, trial and execution. We shall return to Jesus' epic dilemma in our readings for Holy Week. Today we will follow in the steps of Paul and many other Christian theologians across the centuries who have seen in Jesus' prayer to his Father in the garden of Gethsemane a reworking—indeed, overturning—of events in the garden of Eden.

In last week's readings we heard Jesus' warning about the wrong attitude to prayer, which stems from an attitude to life that has lost its heavenly perspective. Because the heavenly way is hard and narrow (Matthew 7:14) and seems to go against the human grain, it is easy for us to disregard the divine voice and attend to the things of the world. We then become vulnerable to temptation.

This is the situation in the garden of Eden. The first human beings are created by God in his image and have the capacity to live according to his will, yet they choose to depart from it. Without any consultation or questioning of God, Eve is taken in by appearances and the relentless logic of the tempter, and betrays the trust that God has placed in her. Adam is entirely passive and simply takes the line of least resistance when Eve offers him the fruit. He is a pathetic figure.

As we have seen, the big questions that we face in life concern our identity and personal worth. Our sense of self-worth is based strongly on a sense of being loved unconditionally, simply for who we are, and it is worked out through struggles with questions about living our life the right way—doing the right things. If we have a strong sense of our identity and self-worth and we make a mistake, we will see it as something out of character that needs fixing; we will feel *guilty* and we will want to make things right. If, on the other hand, we have a fragile and insecure sense of identity and self-worth, we will see the mistake as something that reveals how bad we really are, something that must be hidden lest we be exposed; we will feel *ashamed* and we will try to cover it up.

What happens to Adam and Eve when they eat the fruit is the emergence of a self-consciousness dominated by shame.

There is no sense of a love relationship with God. They cover themselves and they hide. God is disgusted with them, and the relationship is seen to be broken (though not utterly destroyed). We may think that the depiction of God in this story leaves something to be desired: there is a sense of an absent, autocratic, rather tetchy father, which raises some quite difficult theological questions. But this is a story, not a theological treatise, and it describes superbly the state of affairs between God and humanity as it is felt by so many people and as it seems to work itself out in the world. There is suspicion; shame at falling short, which leads to an excessive preoccupation with self; fear of punishment and destruction. In short, there is anxiety and alienation.

In Christ, however, God acted to deal with this alienation, reconciling the world to himself (2 Corinthians 5:19).

This shines through Jesus' prayer in the garden. God was not pleased with Adam's behaviour in Eden, but he is well pleased with Jesus' behaviour in Gethsemane. Unlike Adam, Jesus does not hide from God; he calls out to him. Unlike Adam, Jesus is not preoccupied with his own self-consciousness. Because he is secure in his relationship with his Father, he actually seeks to empty himself, to align himself to his Father's will, as Paul reflects in the famous hymn in Philippians (2:5–11). And, unlike Adam and Eve, but like his mother Mary (Luke 1:34), Jesus engages critically with God. He asks his Father if there is any way he can avoid going to the cross. Jesus may be God's beloved Son, but the interchange between them is very much adult to adult rather than parent to child. Having reached an understanding, Jesus makes a free choice to align himself with God's way; he takes the final steps on the road to the cross.

When Jesus prays '*Abba*', he is demonstrating that our

relationship with God does not have to be one of alienation dominated by shame, but can be one of intimacy where we feel confident enough to ask questions and admit mistakes. It does not have to be one where we are infantilised, but can be one in which God does business with us as the grown-up human beings he has always intended us to become. Jesus shows that, secure in this love relationship and with our eyes open to the difficulty of the challenge and the immensity of the call, it is possible for us to go against the grain and align ourselves with God's will. And because Jesus has come out on the other side of the cross and grave, he shows us that this hard and narrow way leads to life.

Prayer

Abba, you have searched me and known me; it was you who formed my inward parts and knit me together in my mother's womb. I come to you unashamed, trusting in your Son, Jesus.

Tuesday

The promise of the Spirit

'If you love me, you will keep my commandments. And I will ask the Father, and he will give you another Advocate, to be with you for ever. This is the Spirit of truth, whom the world cannot receive, because it neither sees him nor knows him. You know him, because he abides with you, and he will be in you. I will not leave you orphaned; I am coming to you. In a little while the world will no longer see me, but you will see me; because I live, you also will live. On that day you will know that I am in my Father, and you in me, and I in you... Those who love me will keep my word, and my Father will love them, and we will come to them and make our home with them. Whoever does not love me does not keep my words; and the word that you hear is not mine, but is from the Father who sent me. I have said these things to you while I am still with you. But the Advocate, the Holy Spirit, whom the Father will send in my name, will teach you everything, and remind you of all that I have said to you.'
JOHN 14:15–20, 23–26

By his life, death and resurrection, Jesus shows us how things can be between God and human beings. This expansive vision raises our horizons and motivates us to 'lift [our] drooping hands and strengthen [our] weak knees' (Hebrews 12:12). But Jesus is more than an inspirational heroic figure, who gives us hope and whom we strive to emulate. We are not in the business of pulling ourselves up by our own bootstraps while Jesus shouts words of encouragement from the sidelines. Through the prayer of Jesus, *God* is at work transforming the lives of human beings. This transformation is effected by the Holy Spirit.

Paul understands this only too well. As we noted yesterday, Paul found it helpful to think of Jesus as a counterpoint to Adam, turning the tree of death on which he was crucified into a tree of life for us. He explores the idea in both his letter to the Romans and his first letter to the Corinthians, at one point referring to Jesus as 'the last Adam'. Paul says this: '"The first man, Adam, became a living being"; the last Adam became a life-giving spirit' (1 Corinthians 15:45). Adam was created by God, who breathed life into dust, and eventually Adam died. In contrast, says Paul, Jesus died and was raised, and now he gives life to us through the Spirit. In Semitic languages, the ideas of spirit, breath and wind are deeply interconnected. Paul is saying that God inspirited the first Adam with life but that the second Adam inspirits us with life. In John's Gospel we actually have an account of Jesus breathing the Spirit into his followers (20:22).

In our reading for today, from a little earlier in John's Gospel, Jesus promises this Spirit in advance. Notice how he says that the Father will send the Holy Spirit 'in my name'—that is, 'in accordance with my nature'. If we have the Spirit, we have Jesus, even though the human being Jesus of Nazareth has long since departed this earth. When the earthly Jesus goes, the Spirit comes. Of course, the Spirit has been around from the beginning, but the role of the Spirit in the aftermath of the death and raising of Jesus is new. John uses the Greek word *paraklētos*, which can be translated 'advocate', 'helper' or 'comforter'—essentially someone who is on our side.

Notice, too, that the Spirit is described as invisible from a worldly perspective. The Spirit undercuts the values of the world that we considered in last Saturday's reflection, and for its part the world cannot see or just 'doesn't get' the Spirit. In order to perceive and be instructed and prompted by the Spirit, we need an appropriate attitude of attentiveness and an openness to a heavenly perspective.

But, says Jesus, there is more. We are not simply to perceive the Spirit—to benefit from a sense of the presence of Christ with us. We are to *receive* the Spirit. That is, the trinitarian God will inhabit us. Here we get into some really deep and perhaps disturbing waters, for we are talking about a depth of connection between the disciple and the divine that I mentioned in the Introduction—something that might best be described as 'incorporation' or 'union'. After the departure of the earthly Jesus, the coming of the Spirit enables an even closer relationship with his followers. The translation of *paraklētos* as 'comforter' is perhaps misleading, for the Spirit is not like a security blanket—a pale reflection of the departed loved one, something we have to make do with until our absent beloved returns. Instead we find the opposite: the relationship moves up a gear from 'Christ with us' to 'Christ in and through us'—something that Paul refers to when he says, 'We have the mind of Christ' (1 Corinthians 2:16).

The Spirit has been around from the beginning. At his baptism, when the skies were parted, Jesus heard the reassuring voice of his Father, but he also looked up and saw the Spirit, and it came to rest upon him. As we have seen, in Luke's account, Jesus' ministry begins with the proclamation, 'The Spirit of the Lord is upon me' (Luke 4:18), and Jesus is also described as being full of the Holy Spirit and rejoicing in the Holy Spirit (4:1, 14; 10:21). His particular use of *Abba* to address God has been described by some as a sign of 'charismatic intimacy'—a mark not only of an attachment relationship with the Father but also of the indwelling of the Spirit.

So, when Jesus promises the Spirit to his followers, he goes beyond showing us that it is possible for a human being to have an *Abba* relationship with God: he grants us the capacity for this relationship. He promises to breathe life into us. When we say '*Abba*', we are speaking the breath of life.

Prayer

Abba, in whom we live and move and have our being, breathe Christ more deeply into my life.

Wednesday

The coming of the Spirit

But when the fullness of time had come, God sent his Son, born of a woman, born under the law, in order to redeem those who were under the law, so that we might receive adoption as children. And because you are children, God has sent the Spirit of his Son into our hearts, crying, 'Abba! Father!' So you are no longer a slave but a child, and if a child then also an heir, through God.

GALATIANS 4:4–7

In yesterday's reading, John recalled Jesus' promise of the Spirit to his followers on the night he was taken from them. In today's reading from Paul's letter to the Galatians, one of the earliest documents in the New Testament, we see that the promise was fulfilled. In the middle of a complex argument about something else (circumcision), Paul invokes a fact that he knows is accepted as a given by his audience: the Spirit has come, and we know this because, when we pray, we are able to address God as *Abba*. This is not a matter for discussion or debate; it is the common lived experience of the first Christian communities within whose reality all other discussion and debate take place.

Paul's experience agrees with John's recollection of Jesus' promise: if we have the Spirit, we have Jesus, even though the human being Jesus of Nazareth has long since departed this earth. We have Jesus with us and we have Jesus in us. The Greek makes it clear that Paul understands that when a Christian prays *Abba*, it is not simply her response to Christ; it is the Spirit of Christ in her who speaks.

Paul makes sense of this by talking of family connections. Jesus of Nazareth was a human being and is therefore in some sense our brother. His raising from the dead vindicates and exalts him, and by it he is 'declared to be Son of God with power according to the spirit of holiness' (Romans 1:4). This naturally brings benefits for his brothers and sisters, who through the same Spirit are in some sense raised up with him. Human beings therefore have access to the heavenly realm through their connection with Jesus, the Son of God. We too can be called sons and daughters of God, but because Jesus' relationship with the Father is unique, Paul talks of Jesus as God's natural child, and ourselves as liberated slaves who have been adopted by God as his children.

Jesus of Nazareth is our brother because he was a human being—the ultimate human being, in fact. He stands in solidarity with the whole of humanity. With the coming of the Spirit, however, a special connection between the risen Christ and his followers is established. Paul, continuing to play with the family metaphor, describes this as a family resemblance. We haven't simply been incorporated into the heavenly family as adopted children by a legal transaction; through the Spirit an organic process is also at work, in which we actually take on some of the family DNA. This shows itself in certain family characteristics. The first and definitive of these characteristics is our ability to pray, 'Abba'.

In the book of Acts, Luke describes the coming of the Spirit at Pentecost. As with the baptism of Jesus, words can do limited justice to the way that heaven touched earth on that occasion. Dramatic images of fire and wind are used to convey the immense power and dynamism of the experience. Perhaps even more strikingly, there is a portrayal of Peter, changed from a man who wants to distance himself from Jesus and hide in fear from the authorities behind closed doors to a man who is prepared to be counted for Jesus in public, no matter what the cost, and is eloquent in proclaiming him as Lord and Saviour. The Spirit is seen here to be an agent of personal transformation.

The transformation begins in a seemingly small way with the ability of the first Christians to speak new words. These words were not meaningless but allowed them to *communicate* with others in their mother-tongues rather than the lingua franca of common Greek. This is very significant. The first Christians were not engaging in a game of linguistic clever tricks. Rather, they had somehow gained the ability to make an intimate connection with their listeners, and thus to speak heart to heart. Here, as elsewhere in the New Testament (for example, Acts 19:6), it is made very clear that the giving of the Spirit enables a new form of intimate speech—a language of the heart.

This gift of intimate speech is fragile, for it can so easily turn into the piling up of empty phrases that Jesus warned his followers against—a human work rather than a spiritual gift. The church at Corinth seems to have had exactly this problem (1 Corinthians 13), and over the centuries the charismatic Christian tradition has remained highly vulnerable to it. But the gift is also precious and should be deeply cherished. In our reading yesterday, as he stressed the centrality of the love-bond between himself and his followers, Jesus spoke of the importance of 'keeping my words'—and, as we have seen, the word of his love-bond is *Abba*.

Prayer

Abba, Jesus, Spirit, transform my words, that I may speak to others in the language of their hearts.

Christ in you

It is no longer I who live, but it is Christ who lives in me. And the life I now live in the flesh I live by faith in the Son of God, who loved me and gave himself for me.

GALATIANS 2:20

But if Christ is in you, though the body is dead because of sin, the Spirit is life because of righteousness. If the Spirit of him who raised Jesus from the dead dwells in you, he who raised Christ from the dead will give life to your mortal bodies also through his Spirit that dwells in you... For all who are led by the Spirit of God are children of God. For you did not receive a spirit of slavery to fall back into fear, but you have received a spirit of adoption. When we cry, 'Abba! Father!' it is that very Spirit bearing witness with our spirit that we are children of God, and if children, then heirs, heirs of God and joint heirs with Christ—if, in fact, we suffer with him so that we may also be glorified with him.

ROMANS 8:10–11, 14–17

Yesterday's reading about the coming of the Spirit was from chapter 4 of Paul's letter to the Galatians. The first of today's two readings jumps back to a little earlier in this letter. Here Paul makes an amazing statement. He says that he lives no more but that Christ lives in him. This is the clearest statement in the New Testament of the idea that followers of Jesus somehow become Jesus, but Paul's statement is not just about identity: it is about life. When Paul says that Christ lives in us, he does not mean that we are like houses—inanimate objects—inhabited by Christ; he means that Christ's presence in us enables *us* to live. As we saw in Tuesday's reflection, it is as if Christ breathes life into us through the Spirit.

The Spirit is like oxygen breathed into us by Christ, which is then carried in the blood that courses through our arteries to enliven our whole being. Red blood full of oxygen is a powerful symbol of life and has been understood in this way by people from many cultures from earliest times. This respect for blood as a sign of the life force is what lies behind animal sacrifices. The aim is not to hurt or punish the animal but to let its life-giving blood flow freely. A sacrificial death is not defined by the fact that it hurts or is costly (though of course it may be both), but by the fact that it brings life. Jesus himself uses the image of blood sacrifice to describe his own death. He talks of the giving of his life as a pouring out of the blood of the covenant—a covenant that marks our reconciliation with God (Mark 14:24).

Paul mentions the death of Jesus in today's short extract from Galatians. He would have seen the sacrificial overtones of Jesus' bloody death very clearly, and this would have helped him to make sense of it, but, at the end of the day, what touches him is something much more personal. It is the fact that God in Christ loved him enough to go to the cross to make things right between them. The oxygen breathed into him by Jesus, and coursing through his arteries, is love.

In the second of today's readings, from his letter to the Romans, written about five years after Galatians, Paul picks up and develops the idea of adoption that we encountered yesterday. Again, we have the idea of the life-giving Spirit inhabiting the Christian. Again, we have the idea that our ability to call God *Abba* is a sign of the Spirit's presence. But here Paul helpfully refines and clarifies what he is saying. Yes, Christ through the Spirit dwells within us and transforms us into new creations, but the Spirit does not take us over: we are not possessed or colonised. Instead, says Paul, the Spirit works in cooperation with our human spirit. I do not become Christ-like because Christ has somehow jackbooted his way into my life and taken it over. I become Christ-like by a voluntary act of alignment with him and by cooperating with the Spirit in a jointly owned work of personal transformation. Part of what it means to be raised up with Christ to the status of a joint heir is that we become co-workers with God in our own salvation. We remain free and we retain the capacity to go off course, but we have the Spirit as our compass. We are a work in progress but our destination remains clear—conformity to and identity with Christ.

Towards the end of this reading, Paul talks about a key way in which the Christian is aligned with Christ and transformed through the Spirit—by walking the way of the cross that leads through suffering and death to glory. Here we naturally return to the story of Stephen.

Luke tells us that, in life, Stephen was 'a man full of faith and the Holy Spirit' (Acts 6:5), and that he spoke with the Spirit (v. 10). As his death approaches, it also becomes clear that Stephen has gained a heavenly perspective, for, like Jesus at his baptism, he looks up and sees the skies open (7:56). In the midst of his suffering with Christ, Stephen sees 'the Son of Man'—the ultimate human being—glorified as part of the Godhead. Here is the basis of his hope of glory as a human being, and of ours too. It is a glory that has, in fact, been shining in Stephen's life for quite some time, for Luke earlier writes that 'his face was like the face of an angel' (6:15).

As he speaks words of forgiveness to his tormentors,

Stephen seems completely aligned with Christ. He is so like Jesus in his way of undergoing suffering and violent death that he effectively is Jesus, or, to use Paul's words, that he no longer lives but Christ lives in him. Yet Stephen's final words are revealing: 'Lord Jesus, receive my spirit' (Acts 7:59). Stephen is filled with the Spirit; he has walked the way of Christ; he is 'being transformed into the same image from one degree of glory to another' (2 Corinthians 3:18), but right up until the moment of death he also retains his own spirit, and he makes a free choice to offer it to Christ, his firstborn brother. Stephen is a child, not a slave.

Prayer

Abba, may your Spirit lead my spirit into the way of Christ.

Friday

Abide in me
as I abide in you

'I am the true vine, and my Father is the vine-grower. He removes every branch in me that bears no fruit. Every branch that bears fruit he prunes to make it bear more fruit. You have already been cleansed by the word that I have spoken to you. Abide in me as I abide in you. Just as the branch cannot bear fruit by itself unless it abides in the vine, neither can you unless you abide in me. I am the vine, you are the branches. Those who abide in me and I in them bear much fruit, because apart from me you can do nothing. Whoever does not abide in me is thrown away like a branch and withers; such branches are gathered, thrown into the fire, and burned. If you abide in me, and my words abide in you, ask for whatever you wish, and it will be done for you. My Father is glorified by this, that you bear much fruit and become my disciples. As the Father has loved me, so I have loved you; abide in my love. If you keep my commandments, you will abide in my love, just as I have kept my Father's commandments and abide in his love. I have said these things to you so that my joy may be in you, and that your joy may be complete... I appointed you to go and bear fruit, fruit that will last, so that the Father will give you whatever you ask him in my name.'
JOHN 15:1–11, 16B

The fruit of the Spirit is love, joy, peace, patience, kindness, generosity, faithfulness, gentleness, and self-control.
GALATIANS 5:22–23A

If the Spirit lives in us, we become as Christ, secure in the love of our *Abba* and confident to address God as such. Christ breathes life-giving oxygen into our blood and we flourish and grow. What does this flourishing look like?

In John 14 (which we read on Tuesday), Jesus tells his disciples that, through the Spirit, he will come and be both with and in his followers. He will be in them but, he says, they will also be in him. In today's reading, from the following chapter, Jesus picks up this theme and stresses that there is a two-way process at work. He will stay with and in us, enlivening our existence, but we need to remain attached to him. We are not to be passive. As we saw from yesterday's readings, our initial consent and then our continuing co-operation are required.

This is one way that we can understand what the Bible means by 'faith'. I said in the Introduction that faith is not our beliefs about God; it is the relationship of trust with God that we live out. We show our trust in God rather as we would show our trust in a medical practitioner—by giving our consent to his activity in our lives. More than that, we are to work with God rather than doing nothing or working against him. In this respect, trusting God is more like trusting a physiotherapist than trusting a surgeon.

Jesus emphasises that we must stay actively connected to him if we are to continue to flourish. The image of a plant whose vessels supply all its branches with life-giving water and nutrients is very much like the image of red blood, full of oxygen, coursing through vessels to supply all the parts of the body. These two images come together in the wine of the last supper (the 'fruit of the vine'), which Jesus refers to as his blood. These images are vivid, and the take-home message is simple: if you want to stay alive, stick close to Jesus.

This sticking close happens through contemplation of Jesus in prayer. It comes through meditation on the words of Jesus (the first of which is *Abba*), so that they become deeply embedded in our minds and character. It comes, as we saw yesterday, through walking the hard and narrow way of Jesus. It comes through remembering and 'eating and drinking' Christ (John 6:51–58) in the bread and 'fruit of the vine' of Holy Communion. It is about learning, marking and inwardly digesting. If we stick close to Christ in this way, we will flourish.

Jesus talks about this flourishing as the bearing of fruit, and the nature of the fruit we bear indicates who it is who abides in us: 'for each tree is known by its own fruit' (Luke 6:44a). Here we have another picture of family resemblance: we are brothers and sisters of Christ and children of God; we are branches of Christ, planted and tended by God in his vineyard—and if we flourish, we will be productive.

Paul picks up the image in our second reading, reminding us that this fruit grows as the natural outcome of our connection with Christ through the activity of the Spirit. We can't contrive the fruit through our own efforts, but, if we make sure we stick close to Jesus, it will develop naturally. Paul helpfully spells out what the fruit actually is: it is a Christ-like character marked by virtues, the first and most important of which is love. The Spirit is essentially love, so it is not surprising that the first of its fruits is love.

The fruits of the Spirit are not simply signs of the flourishing of individual Christians. They are for the building up of the community and for making Christ's presence felt in the world. It is in the context of community and mission that Jesus tells his followers to ask the Father for whatever they wish or need. This open-handed relationship is possible because we are to ask 'in my name' (v. 16): that is, we are to ask in accordance with the nature of Jesus. Our petitions are to be aligned with his, and in this way we approach God as *Abba*.

Just as they are in a healthy human family, the relationships within the Trinity and between the trinitarian God and those who pray to him are not cool and distant, but warm, intimate, even playful. Jesus says that where the Spirit is active in its work of love, the second fruit on Paul's list will bubble up and overflow. This is the wonderful fruit of joy.

Prayer

Abba, may I rest in the love of your Son, Jesus, and joyfully bear spiritual fruit in his name.

Too deep for words

Likewise the Spirit helps us in our weakness; for we do not know how to pray as we ought, but that very Spirit intercedes with sighs too deep for words. And God, who searches the heart, knows what is the mind of the Spirit, because the Spirit intercedes for the saints according to the will of God. We know that all things work together for good for those who love God, who are called according to his purpose. For those whom he foreknew he also predestined to be conformed to the image of his Son, in order that he might be the firstborn within a large family.

ROMANS 8:26–29

Too many words. On this last day of the first week of Lent, it may do us good to have a reflection with fewer words and more space.

Words are important but, as we have seen, the language of the Spirit is a language of the heart. This is good because there are many times in our lives when we do not know what to say—when, indeed, no words will be adequate. What do you say to a bereaved friend, overcome with grief? Or to a relative awaiting the results of tests for cancer? Or to a colleague who has just given birth to a baby with severe disabilities? You try to reach out with a language of the heart but you may end up saying nothing very much at all. And how do you pray for people in these situations? Here we have the promise of the Spirit as our helper, to make Christ's presence felt in the silence between two people and to pray when there are no adequate words to form a prayer.

For some, words literally won't come because they are too young to speak, or they do not speak the language of the country in which they find themselves, or they have a physical or mental impairment that prevents them from forming words, or they have lost the power of framing thoughts, perhaps as the result of dementia.

The repetitive basic sounds that make up the word *Abba* are the sounds of infant babblings, of those whose speech is ill-formed, of those whose capacity for sensible language has fled—the first and the last sounds. They are the sounds of foreigners who babble. The word 'barbarian' comes from the Greek *barbaros*, used to indicate anyone who was a foreigner or not a member of the city-state of Athens. These outsiders were recognised and stigmatised by their babbling.

Yet Jesus is the man who welcomes outsiders and rejoices in the utterances of babies: 'You have hidden these things from the wise and the intelligent and have revealed them to infants' (Matthew 11:25; Luke 10:21). In response to the priests and scribes who complain about the children shouting 'Hosanna' in the temple, he says, 'Have you never read, "Out of the mouths of infants and nursing babies you have prepared praise for yourself"?' (Matthew 21:16).

There is thus something wonderfully subversive about praying or even breathing the simple sounds of *Abba*. There is solidarity with those who cannot speak; there is solidarity with the outsiders who are welcomed by Christ into his kingdom; there is an opening of the heart to the language of God; there is a relaxing on to the breath of the Spirit as words fail us, as they surely will for us all at the end of our earthly lives.

In today's reading from Romans, Paul says something else. The work of the Spirit, cooperating with our spirit, helping us when we have no words, is all for a greater purpose. We are to become 'icons of Christ' or, to put it more prosaically, to grow up just like our big brother who first called God *Abba*.

Prayer

Abba.

Week 2

MAY YOUR NAME BE HELD HOLY

We are meant to begin our lives cradled in the arms of those who love and care for us and, says Jesus, it is also fitting for us to begin our prayer in this way. Secure in our relationship with a God who is our first and last caregiver, who enjoys and delights in us, who works in cooperation with us, and into whose family we are welcomed as beloved children, we can move on and begin the work of prayer. This life-giving and liberating relationship has been modelled for us by the man Jesus of Nazareth, whose relationship with God was intimate, free and full of joy; it was made possible by his death and raising, which opened the way to heaven for us (Hebrews 4:14–16); and it is offered to us through the Spirit of the risen Jesus Christ.

When we say, '*Abba* Father', we both express and claim this relationship; it is all bound in one little word, one little sigh, one little breath.

But this is astonishing! We are talking not simply about the One who loves and cares for us but the One who created the cosmos, whose mind conceived everything from the workings of the smallest sub-atomic particles to the myriad stars and galaxies whirling in space. We are talking about the One whose breath not only enlivens our spirits but also sustains the universe. We are talking about the One who is more powerful than any nuclear reactor—and we are talking *to* this One.

Lest we forget this, the next words in the Lord's Prayer, as given to us by Luke, are all about the sacred, holy nature of the One we are bold enough to address as 'Father'. In this respect, the Lord's Prayer resembles other Jewish prayers at the time of Jesus, which often incorporate the idea of God's name being 'held holy' (NJB) or 'hallowed' (NRSV). For instance, the Aramaic *Kaddish* begins:

Magnified and sanctified
may his great name be
in the world that he created.

These words seem to be a reminder to the people who are praying that they have been created by God and that their lives are meant to reflect God's glory. In Judaism this is understood to be expressed in being faithful in prayer and in keeping the Ten Commandments (Mark 10:20).

The Ten Commandments begin with the statement, 'I am the LORD your God, who brought you out of the land of Egypt, out of the house of slavery' (Exodus 20:2; Deuteronomy 5:6). This is a mark of God's covenant relationship with his people, and it sets his demands in the context of a pre-existing relationship of trust. God is reminding his people that he saved them in the past and so they can trust him to protect them now and in the future.

However, God isn't simply saying 'Remember me—your God who helped you last time you were in trouble?' He makes a point of identifying himself with the words, 'I am the LORD.'

Whenever we find the word LORD in capital letters in English Bibles, it is a translation of the Hebrew word YHWH, which is actually a non-word—impossible to pronounce because it is made up exclusively of consonants, with no indication of what vowels might be fitted in between them. This is because the name of the One Living God is considered so sacred in Judaism that it is never uttered. When read aloud from the Torah, a substitute word is spoken each time YHWH is encountered—the word *Adonai* (in English, 'the Lord').

This great respect and awe for the name of God reminds us that God cannot be tamed, owned or understood as an object—even an object to be worshipped and adored. He comes before all created objects and is their origin. The psychologist William James said that a true sense of the divine feels 'primal' or 'primordial': 'You must go before the foreground of existence and reach down to that curious sense of the whole residual cosmos as an everlasting presence.'[7] God has been there from the first. Indeed, God defines what we mean by the first: 'I am He; I am the first, and I am the last' (Isaiah 48:12b).

To acknowledge that God is first, and the source of everything else in the universe, is to acknowledge that he is not just our redeemer but our creator. This is a truth that fills some of the writers of the Old Testament with wonder and praise (see, for instance, Psalm 19:1a: 'The heavens are telling the glory of God'). Others respond more soberly by reminding us of the 'otherness' of God. When Job is confronted with God's creative power, he realises just how wide is the gulf between the human and divine mind (Job 42:1–6). We see this theme in Isaiah, too:

For my thoughts are not your thoughts, nor are your ways my ways, says the LORD. For as the heavens are higher than the earth, so are my ways higher than your ways and my thoughts than your thoughts.
Isaiah 55:8–9

The second line of the Lord's Prayer calls our attention to the fact that the God who has revealed himself in Jesus is so holy, and so 'wholly other' from us, that we must never lose our sense of astonished wonder at his grace in granting us a secure and intimate relationship with him. This is not a relationship with some sort of idealised human parent but with the primordial cosmic LORD. Even before *Abba*, he is Alpha. Or, to put it in Jesus' words, 'Before Abraham was, I am' (John 8:58).

It's me! Do not be afraid

By this time the boat, battered by the waves, was far from the land, for the wind was against them. And early in the morning he came walking toward them on the lake. But when the disciples saw him walking on the lake, they were terrified, saying, 'It is a ghost!' And they cried out in fear. But immediately Jesus spoke to them and said, 'Take heart, it is I; do not be afraid.' Peter answered him, 'Lord, if it is you, command me to come to you on the water.' He said, 'Come.' So Peter got out of the boat, started walking on the water, and came toward Jesus. But when he noticed the strong wind, he became frightened, and beginning to sink, he cried out, 'Lord, save me!' Jesus immediately reached out his hand and caught him, saying to him, 'You of little faith, why did you doubt?' When they got into the boat, the wind ceased. And those in the boat worshipped him, saying, 'Truly you are the Son of God.'
MATTHEW 14:24–33

God is wholly other, all-knowing and all-powerful. He created the worlds and he set the laws of nature in place. Indeed, he acts through these laws to sustain the created order. God is sovereign over the material stuff of this world and the forces of nature. We, on the other hand, are made of material stuff and live in accordance with the forces of nature. At best we manage them or harness them to our advantage; at worst we are at their mercy.

Those of us who inhabit comfortable urban environments can easily forget this fact. Our food comes from shops whose shelves are always well stocked. We expect to be able to travel with ease by car or public transport, which shield us from the effects of the elements. The nearest we come to concern about nature is checking the weather forecast to see if we should take an umbrella with us when we go out or if we could have a barbecue at the weekend. We get indignant when snow disrupts our plans, complaining that the authorities have lost control of the situation.

People who live in the countryside and work the land, or inhabit parts of the world where the effects of nature have a direct impact on them, have quite a different attitude. Here there is much greater respect for the forces of sunshine, wind and rain, for earth and sea. These people do not delude themselves that human beings have control over nature. This perhaps explains why atheism is more common in big cities than in rural communities. When you are close to nature, you are also aware of the divine—'that curious sense of the whole residual cosmos as an everlasting presence'.[8]

When nature shows itself at its most dramatic or ferocious, we respond in awe. Awe is an emotion called up by experiences that are immense in scale and beyond our comprehension. The US government used a military tactic called 'Shock and Awe' to subdue the population of Baghdad in the last Gulf War: the aim was to 'overload an adversary's perceptions and understanding of events'.[9]

When we are in awe of something or someone, we feel small, incapable of thought or action, and often we feel afraid. This is also our natural response to the power and presence of the living God. In today's reading, the disciples in their little boat on the Sea of Galilee clearly feel something similar. First, they are fighting a losing battle against a storm, far from the shore and 'battered by the waves'. They are faced with the immensity of nature. Then they see something uncanny—someone appearing to walk on the surface of the water. Their perceptions are overloaded and they are terrified.

Straight away, though, Jesus (for it is he) tells them to have courage and identifies himself. Like a parent comforting a child having a nightmare, he says, 'It's OK—it's me!'

When we phone those closest to us, we don't bother telling them our names. Instead we say, 'It's me'—or, if we think they might be worried about who is calling them late at night, we may say, 'It's only me.' Jesus is using that sort of intimate language here (although, as we shall see in tomorrow's reading, it is language that is highly charged with a greater significance), and he continues by telling his disciples not to be afraid. Jesus knows that their natural response will be fear and he assures them that there is nothing to be afraid of.

Peter then does something remarkable. He makes a conscious and free decision to direct himself towards Jesus. This is the beginning of prayer—an intentional turning to the One who will do us good. It is all that we need to do. God helps us with the rest. We have already seen that when we do not know what to pray, the Spirit helps us in our weakness. Here we see that when Peter's faith and footing become unsure, when he is in danger of being overwhelmed by the waves and his own fear, Jesus catches him, raises him up out of the water and pulls him into the boat. The typical dynamic of Jesus is upwards and onwards, and, if we let him, he will take us with him.

Jesus shows himself to have power and authority over the forces of nature. It seems to come so naturally to him that he doesn't remark on it at all, being more concerned to comfort his frightened followers—and this is the point. Nature is awesome; God is awesome; yet, in the midst of shock and awe, one who has authority over nature says gently, 'It's OK.'

As the wind and waves die down and the disciples' feelings of awe and fear dissipate, they are able to reflect on their experience. Somehow, in a way they cannot fully understand, they realise that in having to do with the man Jesus, they are having to do with the LORD their God. So again they do what comes naturally: they worship him.

Prayer

Abba, as you hold me in your arms, may I hold your name holy.

Monday

I am. Do not fear

Thus says the LORD, the King of Israel and his Redeemer, the LORD of hosts: I am the first and I am the last; besides me there is no god. Who is like me? Let them proclaim it, let them declare and set it forth before me. Who has announced from of old the things to come? Let them tell us what is yet to be. Do not fear, or be afraid; have I not told you from of old and declared it? You are my witnesses! Is there any god besides me? There is no other rock; I know not one.

ISAIAH 44:6–8

It is in Isaiah 40—55 that we find the most radical statements of monotheism in the Old Testament. The LORD is unique: there is nothing and no one like him. He is not just the best of a whole crowd of gods; there are no other gods at all. Indeed, there never have been. The LORD has been there from the beginning, he sees all that is to come, and he will be there at the last.

Today's reading was written around the time of the return home to Jerusalem of the people of God from their Babylonian exile in the sixth century BC. There is a great sense of joy and anticipation that the LORD, who saved the people from the Egyptians so many years before, has acted in accordance with his nature as redeemer and is about to release them from the Babylonians. The LORD can be trusted to keep his word. We saw in Sunday's reading from last week that the LORD was a rock for David. Here, many centuries later, he is a rock for the exiled people in Babylon.

In this part of Isaiah we also find an emphasis on God as creator of the universe, and we find scorn at the idea of idolatry—worshipping the creature instead of the creator and thinking of God as an object. Amid all this reverence and awe for the power and otherness of God, we also find a very particular form of words with which God refers to himself: 'I AM' or 'I AM he' (in Hebrew *'anî hû'*). This distinctive phrase is almost exclusive to this part of Isaiah;[10] it emphasises the LORD's holiness and sovereignty over the cosmos, reminding us that he 'was and is and is to come' (Revelation 4:8).

By the time of Jesus, the Hebrew Bible had been translated into Greek. In Greek, the same words (*egō eimi*) were used to translate both 'I AM' and 'It's me'. So, in the Greek New Testament, whenever somebody says 'It's me!' it could actually mean 'I AM he'. It's almost like a pun. John makes a lot of this pun in his Gospel. He draws our attention to Jesus' words, 'Before Abraham was it's me/I AM he' (John 8:58) and, in his account of the arrest in the garden, he tells us that when the soldiers, police, and religious leaders say that they are looking for Jesus of Nazareth, Jesus responds, 'It's me/ I AM he.' 'When Jesus said to them, "I am he," they stepped back and fell to the ground' (John 18:6). It's as if, on hearing these words, people who had assumed that Jesus was just a troublesome religious or political fanatic momentarily caught a glimpse of the cosmic reality of his true identity.

So, in yesterday's reading, that homely, intimate 'It's me!' which must have brought such comfort to his disciples, can also be understood as revealing the amazing truth that Jesus himself is the LORD. He walks on the water, he stills the storm and he says, 'I AM he.' In today's reading, the LORD reveals himself and, at the same time, urges his people not to be afraid, for he is with them and can be trusted to save them.

This is, of course, exactly what Jesus of Nazareth did as he walked on the Sea of Galilee.

God is terrible and holy, and his name must be hallowed. The forces of nature over which he has command can be terrifying. The sheer complexity of this world can threaten to overwhelm our little lives with chaos. But, says Jesus, 'It's OK. I—the living God who made you—am here in solidarity with you as your friend and brother. Don't be afraid.'

Prayer

Creator God, you who uphold the cosmos and have reached out and upheld us in Jesus, may your name be held holy.

Show us the Father

In the beginning was the Word, and the Word was with God, and the Word was God. He was in the beginning with God. All things came into being through him, and without him not one thing came into being. What has come into being in him was life, and the life was the light of all people. The light shines in the darkness, and the darkness did not overcome it.

There was a man sent from God, whose name was John. He came as a witness to testify to the light, so that all might believe through him. He himself was not the light, but he came to testify to the light. The true light, which enlightens everyone, was coming into the world. He was in the world, and the world came into being through him; yet the world did not know him. He came to what was his own, and his own people did not accept him. But to all who received him, who believed in his name, he gave power to become children of God, who were born, not of blood or of the will of the flesh or of the will of man, but of God.

And the Word became flesh and lived among us, and we have seen his glory, the glory as of a father's only son, full of grace and truth. (John testified to him and cried out, 'This was he of whom I said, "He who comes after me ranks ahead of me because he was before me."') From his fullness we have all received, grace upon grace. The law indeed was given through Moses; grace and truth came through Jesus Christ. No one has ever seen God. It is God the only Son, who is close to the Father's heart, who has made him known.

JOHN 1:1–18

Psalm 19 begins, 'The heavens are telling the glory of God', but the beginning of John's Gospel claims that Jesus is the glory of God. Here John is reflecting on the incomprehensible wonder that we explored in the last two readings: human beings, who are so different from God that they cannot see him and dare not name him, are yet able to know him because he himself became a human being.

John has not arrived at this conclusion by sitting in an armchair and thinking what a jolly good idea it would be if the LORD became incarnate. It is quite the reverse. The conclusion that in Jesus 'the fullness of God was pleased to dwell' (Colossians 1:19) has been forced upon him. He has seen and lived alongside Jesus of Nazareth and, for John, the only possible explanation that can do justice to the glory of Jesus' life, death and raising is that this man is the LORD God.

God has been there from the first and we are recent arrivals in the cosmos; through his Word, God created all flesh, including us; God is the source of light and we are in need of enlightenment; God inhabits the infinite heavenly places beyond the skies and we inhabit this finite world. Yet in Jesus God has broken down all these barriers. He entered human time and space in first-century Palestine; he took on the constraints of human nature (that is, 'flesh'); as a human being, he brought divine light to shine in the darkest corners of human existence, 'seeking out and saving the lost' (Luke 19:10).

Above all, says John, Jesus' task on this earth was to enable people 'to become children of God'. It is exactly the same point that Paul makes many times in his letters, as we saw last week, but here John starts to explore the question of why God would want to do this. He tells us that God is simply being true to his own nature. The creator and sustainer of the cosmos is not a cold genius, not simply a cosmic 'everlasting presence',[11] but a being with a 'heart' who, in some deeply mysterious way, exists in a loving relationship with himself.

This is not narcissism: God is not a self-absorbed, closed system of 'Me, Myself and I'. John tells us that the love of God cannot help but overflow outwards. As we have already seen, the typical dynamic of Jesus is upwards and onwards as he pulls us toward the Godhead, but this itself is part of a bigger picture: the dynamic of the whole Godhead is outward and overflowing, hospitable and welcoming. It is from God's fullness that we receive 'grace upon grace'. This grace invites our response in faith, a living of our lives in accordance with the nature of Christ—what John calls 'believing in his name'. Notice that it also involves receiving with grace the hospitality that has been offered with grace, something that is beautifully expressed elsewhere in the New Testament: 'Listen! I am standing at the door, knocking; if you hear my voice and open the door, I will come in to you and eat with you, and you with me' (Revelation 3:20).

Unlike Moses, who was a messenger carrying a verbal summary of God's commands, Jesus is the everlasting Word of God, there from the beginning as part of God's primordial nature, not talking about grace, but *being* grace and truth. He can do this because he is, if you like, a chip off the old block, the beloved child of his *Abba*.

Prayer

Word of God, there from the beginning, made flesh for us, bringing us grace upon grace, may your name be held holy.

Enthroned on the praises of Israel

Ascribe to the LORD, O heavenly beings,
ascribe to the LORD glory and strength.
Ascribe to the LORD the glory of his name;
worship the LORD in holy splendour.
The voice of the LORD is over the waters;
the God of glory thunders,
the LORD, over mighty waters.
The voice of the LORD is powerful;
the voice of the LORD is full of majesty.
The voice of the LORD breaks the cedars;
the LORD breaks the cedars of Lebanon.
He makes Lebanon skip like a calf,
and Sirion like a young wild ox.
The voice of the LORD flashes forth flames of fire.
The voice of the LORD shakes the wilderness;
the LORD shakes the wilderness of Kadesh.
The voice of the LORD causes the oaks to whirl,
and strips the forest bare;
and in his temple all say, 'Glory!'
The LORD sits enthroned over the flood;
the LORD sits enthroned as king for ever.
May the LORD give strength to his people!
May the LORD bless his people with peace!

PSALM 29

In yesterday's reading we saw that we have received 'grace upon grace' and been given 'power to become the children of God'. We also saw that God's gracious act, in entering the natural created order in Jesus, flows from his eternal nature. He desires to be in a relationship of cooperation with human beings. This is what covenants are all about, involving a two-way commitment: 'They shall be my people and I will be their God' (Jeremiah 24:7b). One aspect of this relationship of grace that we enjoy with God is the privilege of joining with him in his creative work of sustaining and redeeming the world. God's grace extends to allowing us—indeed, inviting us—to become his assistants.

Apart from being astonishing, this is tremendously affirming. How often have we heard small children calling out 'Let me help!' to busy parents who might get the job done more quickly without them? How tempting it is to ignore that cry if you are in a hurry! Yet, if you set aside the agenda of getting the job done quickly, and let a child really help and contribute something to an enterprise, you will be rewarded by his evident pleasure and often surprised by the way he rises to the occasion. They seem to rise in stature, to grow in dignity.

This is exactly what God does with us. He doesn't need us but he chooses to involve us—and we find that, in the process, we have risen to the occasion and grown to become more fully human.

We are perhaps best used to this idea in the context of mission—'being God's hands and feet in the world', to paraphrase St Teresa of Avila—but it is more fundamentally true in the area of prayer. We pray in union with Christ through the power of the Spirit, and our prayer is directed to the Father. Part of our union with Christ is a joining in with his work of prayer. Christ prays for the world, constantly turning to the Father with the world on his heart.[12] Christ is our great high priest (Hebrews 4:14–15) and, through the overflowing fullness of God's grace, when we pray for the needs of the world we are participating in his priestly work. We are not, as it were, whistling in the dark (though it may feel like that at times); we are jumping aboard a magnificent bandwagon of prayer driven by Christ himself.

In prayer we also give praise to God, and this too can be seen as a joining in with his work. This is perhaps a strange idea, for surely God doesn't praise himself? Yet, from earliest times in many cultures, there was an instinctive belief that, in praising God, the people were somehow 'helping' him. Scholars describe it as a belief that praise empowers the one who is praised; that in praising God, the people are invigorating him, realigning themselves in relation to him and participating in the divine act of sustaining the cosmos. This is fundamentally a good instinct, although it can easily be misunderstood. It's not that God needs our praises; he is neither weak nor narcissistic and in need of 'bigging up'. Rather, God's creative and sustaining fullness overflows, so that it is possible for us to be caught up in it, into a giant and joyful 'Yay!'

In our reading for today—a wonderful outpouring of praise to the LORD from the very earliest days of Israel—this instinct of praise as being supportive of God feels strong. The idea of supporting God can be found elsewhere in the Psalms. For instance, in Psalm 22 the people are described as holding God up, with their praises as his 'throne' (v. 3). There is not yet any sense of God's revelation in Jesus, but it is anticipated in the strong sense of God's grace; the people who sing the psalm participate in God's fullness as ruler of the universe and have authority over all sorts of 'heavenly beings'.[13] Their hope and expectation is that, as a result, they will be blessed with God's strength and his peace.

When we hold God's name holy in prayer, we too are caught up in this tradition. We remember and pay due attention to God's power and holiness. That makes it more real in our lives, giving us an attitude of reverence. So, as we do this, an eternal truth is made real for us here and now, and we—weak creatures though we are—find that in our praises God's work is advanced.

Prayer

All-powerful God, as we join, in wonder, with Christ in prayer for your world, may your name be held holy.

Blessed be the Lord the God of Israel, who has come to his people and set them free

---

Then Moses told his father-in-law all that the LORD had done to Pharaoh and to the Egyptians for Israel's sake, all the hardship that had beset them on the way, and how the LORD had delivered them. Jethro rejoiced for all the good that the LORD had done to Israel, in delivering them from the Egyptians. Jethro said, 'Blessed be the LORD, who has delivered you from the Egyptians and from Pharaoh. Now I know that the LORD is greater than all gods, because he delivered the people from the Egyptians, when they dealt arrogantly with them.'

EXODUS 18:8–11

In Monday's reading we saw that, by the time of the return from the Babylonian exile in the sixth century BC, there was a clear understanding that the LORD is the only God. This understanding seems to have developed slowly. In very early times, the Jewish people probably understood the LORD as their tribal or national God, special to them but jostling for position against other gods. Then they came to see the LORD as the only true God. Finally they realised that he wasn't 'a god' at all, not even the best of all the gods, but he was uniquely himself, the first cause of everything else in creation, with whom no other beings could be compared.

Our reading today is taken from an early time in the history of Israel, and so we find Jethro talking of the LORD as 'greater than all the gods'. This isn't a belief he has held for very long. It's a conclusion that he has just reached in the light of what his son-in-law Moses has told him about the people of Israel's escape from Egypt.

The escape from Pharaoh and his troops is a dramatic story in which, against the odds, a small and enslaved people survive the onslaught of a mighty military power. Egypt is afflicted by a series of natural disasters, culminating in the death of the firstborn in each family (Exodus 7—12); the people of Israel leave Egypt and journey into the inhospitable desert, yet they are guided by a strange cloud formation and flaming night sky (13:21–22). Most amazing of all, as they face the pursuing Egyptian army across the Red Sea, the tide turns and engulfs their enemy (ch. 14). They continue their wilderness journey, which is full of hardships, but, when they are near to starvation, mysterious plant life appears to nourish them (ch. 16) and they find a source of clean water (ch. 17) to refresh them.

There are various ways in which we could make sense of all this. We might think that luck was on the side of the Israelites. We might think that Moses and his assistants were cunning and resourceful leaders. We might think that the Jews are a very resilient people with an extraordinarily strong survival instinct. We might think any of these things, but Jethro chooses to say and to think something different. He chooses to attribute the events to God's plan. The LORD has liberated his people and provided for them.

Jethro takes an 'intentional stance': that is, he positions himself towards the One whom he believes has done his people good and, he hopes, will continue to do him good. He is acting in the same way as Peter did when he directed himself towards Jesus as he saw him walking on the water. Jethro is acknowledging the lordship of this One over the forces of nature and of human principalities and powers. Earlier I suggested that an intentional turning or positioning towards God is the beginning of prayer. Here Jethro makes this clear, for he doesn't simply say that he has come to see the events in a particular light, but he first rejoices and says, 'Blessed be the LORD' (in Hebrew, *Bārak Adonai*). Jethro's 'coming to see' is expressed as a prayer.

This is also the beginning of prayer in another sense: scholars think that Jethro's prayer is one of the earliest prayers in the Old Testament. As people came to understand the moral goodness and power of God, and as they gained a sense that he was in charge of the universe and had a providential plan for his people, their natural response was to bless his name. In this, the earliest from of Hebrew prayer, they seemed cautious about addressing God directly. Instead they asserted truths about his nature. Nevertheless, these truths were in the form not of cool creeds but, rather, of warm joyful blessings.

Those of us who pray Morning Prayer regularly will know that the Song of Zechariah (Luke 1:68–79) is a central part of this service. It begins:

Blessed be the Lord the God of Israel,
who has come to his people and set them free.
He has raised up for us a mighty Saviour,
born of the house of his servant David.

COMMON WORSHIP

From very early in the history of the church, Christians wanted to begin the day by asserting the holiness, power and providence of God's saving act in Jesus, by blessing his name in this way, using the ancient Jewish *Bārak Adonai* form. In doing so, they began each day by taking an 'intentional stance' towards the One they knew had done and would continue to do them good.

Yesterday's reading asserted the powerful and holy nature of God; today's reading takes events and interprets them in the light of the powerful and holy nature of God. When we hold God's name holy, we are choosing to embrace a certain attitude to the whole cosmos and the events of our daily lives. This is the attitude that God is in charge, that God is good, and therefore we have hope.

Prayer

As we rejoice in the gift of this new day, so may the light of your presence, O God,
set our hearts on fire with love for you; now and forever.[14]

May your name be held holy.

Friday

I will trust,
and will not be afraid

You will say in that day:
I will give thanks to you, O LORD,
for though you were angry with me,
your anger turned away,
and you comforted me.
Surely God is my salvation;
I will trust, and will not be afraid,
for the LORD GOD is my strength and my might;
he has become my salvation.
With joy you will draw water from the wells of salvation.
And you will say in that day:
Give thanks to the LORD,
call on his name;
make known his deeds among the nations;
proclaim that his name is exalted.
Sing praises to the LORD, for he has done gloriously;
let this be known in all the earth.
Shout aloud and sing for joy, O royal Zion,
for great in your midst is the Holy One of Israel.
ISAIAH 12

The way we behave reflects the way we see ourselves and
the world. When I was training as a clinical psychologist, I
was taught that the problem for people with mental health
conditions is not their 'abnormal' behaviour and feelings, but

the way that they see themselves and the world. The way they feel and act is usually entirely reasonable in the light of their perceptions, but it's those perceptions that are so often distorted or self-destructive. For instance, a young woman may avoid social engagements because she sees herself as hateful. Her primary problem is that she has an abnormal view of herself and other people. Her feelings of misery and her reclusive behaviour are secondary and follow on naturally from her perception. Over years of clinical practice, I have generally found this principle to be true.

If we see the world as a place where God is in charge and we see God as good and providential, our behaviour will reflect this perception. If I see God as trustworthy, then I can dare to trust him. One way of daring to trust is to give thanks. So, the act of holding God's name holy both expresses and makes more real a certain type of relationship. Thanksgiving implies trust.

In today's reading we find a form of prayer that is both later in origin than the one we considered yesterday and a little different from it. This is a prayer of 'thanksgiving' rather than 'blessing', and the crucial difference compared with Jethro's prayer is that it is directed towards God, not simply spoken about him. It's as if, instead of shyly referring to God with downcast eyes, the people have come to feel that they can turn, look upwards and address him directly. I see that God is trustworthy, I can dare to trust him, and so I can even aspire to an 'I–thou' rather than an 'I–him' relationship with him.

But this isn't simple. The world often feels hostile, I often feel weak and inadequate, and events can seem meaningless. On top of that, I am only human and the LORD is the LORD. So, trusting God is an act of faith on my part, and it involves a conscious act of will. Our reading says, '*I will* trust', '*I will* give thanks', '*I will* not be afraid', translating a Hebrew tense that indicates an intention to act or an involvement in an act that is not yet fully complete. A similar act of will is something that is required of people who are in the process of being liberated from distorted or self-destructive ways of seeing the world. As the young woman in my earlier example becomes open to the possibility that she may not be as hateful as she had thought, she will need to test it out by coming into contact with others. The first steps in this process—perhaps meeting an acquaintance for coffee in a quiet place—will take a tremendous act of will (and trust in her therapist) on her part. But if she perseveres she is likely to experience a sense of success and affirmation, and a lessening of her misery. More fundamentally, something of her full identity will be made real.

When we decide to turn to God in thanksgiving, when we determine to trust and not to be afraid, as he has again and again invited us to do, something of his nature is made real in us.

This is a conscious choice, not an unconscious delusion. It's not that the world is one way and we unwittingly believe some kind of fairy story about a loving and powerful God to help us get by. With eyes open, we choose to place our faith in God by asserting his holiness, attributing events to his providence, trusting him where things cannot be easily explained, and obeying his command to cast away fear and anxiety.

This act of faith becomes more real as others join with us. It is, in part, an invitation to the whole community of faith. So, our reading for today moves from describing the prayer of one person to instructing all the people to join in. Notice how, as the people turn to God in this intentional attitude of trust, he is made real in their midst. Also, while the reading is about an act of will, the feeling that comes from it is one of great joy. The way we see the world affects the way we act, and, when we act, our feelings change. We trust God, we give him thanks and we find that great joy emerges.

We see this supremely in the prayer of Jesus: 'At that same hour Jesus rejoiced in the Holy Spirit and said, "I thank you, Father, Lord of heaven and earth, because you have hidden these things from the wise and the intelligent and have revealed them to infants; yes, Father, for such was your gracious will"' (Luke 10:21; see Matthew 11:25–26).

Here, Jesus looks at the cities that have rejected him and the humble folk who have accepted him, choosing to see this as consistent with the nature of the God he has preached in the Beatitudes. As he consciously looks heavenwards and thanks God for his grace, he is filled with joy. He holds God's name holy by acknowledging his sovereignty over the cosmos. But, filled with the Spirit, he slips something else in too, and he says it twice—*Abba*.

Prayer

Abba, Lord of heaven and earth, we will trust and will not be afraid. May your name be held holy.

Saturday

Too wonderful for me

O LORD, our Sovereign,
how majestic is your name in all the earth!
You have set your glory above the heavens.
Out of the mouths of babes and infants
you have founded a bulwark because of your foes,
to silence the enemy and the avenger.
When I look at your heavens, the work of your fingers,
the moon and the stars that you have established;
what are human beings that you are mindful of them,
mortals that you care for them?
Yet you have made them a little lower than God,
and crowned them with glory and honour.
You have given them dominion over the works of your hands;
you have put all things under their feet,
all sheep and oxen,
and also the beasts of the field,
the birds of the air, and the fish of the sea,
whatever passes along the paths of the seas.
O LORD, our Sovereign,
how majestic is your name in all the earth!
PSALM 8

We come to the last day of the second week in Lent and, as we did last week, we pause.

We enter into the sense of awe expressed by the psalmist as he holds God's name holy and considers the stark contrast between the immensity of God as creator of the cosmos and the insignificance of individual human beings. As we have seen, awe tends to make us feel tiny, so the psalmist is full of wonder that the awesome LORD seems to be attentive to and to care for creatures so small in scale and so different in nature.

We are reminded that this is all about God. Human beings exist because God holds us in mind and we flourish because he loves us: 'In this is love, not that we loved God but that he loved us' (1 John 4:10a). We have our place in the world because God has given it to us—indeed, raised us up beyond what we should expect as fleshly creatures. He has done this through his grace, permitting us to participate in his work through our prayer and to cooperate in making real his purposes in the world.

There is one more paradox on which to ponder. In the midst of all this majesty, little babies appear! The Hebrew is hard to translate but it seems to be indicating that from the speech of these little ones comes something that will stand unshakeably against the powers of darkness. As we saw last week, Jesus himself quoted Psalm 8 directly in response to the children's playful acclamation of him in the temple (Matthew 21:16), and was surely influenced by it in the prayer of thanksgiving that we considered yesterday. He reminds his listeners that God reveals himself both to children and through the lips of children and babbling infants at the breast. Here, cosmic *Adonai* is received and named as intimate *Abba*, and, as we have seen, where the cosmic and intimate meet in Jesus, a company of thugs and soldiers fall to the ground in fear and a storm is stilled.

Prayer

Father, may your name be held holy.

Week 3

YOUR KINGDOM COME

'We'll be waiting here till kingdom come.' This glum expression, often to be heard at bus stops and the like, essentially means 'It's never going to happen.' There is a very strong idea embedded in our culture that 'the kingdom' is a future event that has been promised, rather like the events on the bus company timetable, but will in fact never materialise. It looks very much as if this particular bus is not coming. We could hang around and wait for it but, given that we've been waiting so long already, we might as well get a taxi or just give up and go back home.

But if 'the kingdom' were to come, what would it look like. How would we know? What are we actually waiting for?

If we are to pray 'Your kingdom come' with any integrity, we need to have thought about such things. This week we will explore the nature of God's kingdom by posing the questions 'When, where, what, how and who?' Continuing with the bus analogy, we'll be asking, 'When is the bus due? Where is the bus stop? What kind of bus is it? How can I get a ticket?' and only then beginning to wonder, 'Who is the driver?'

These sorts of questions make sense in the light of Jesus' proclamation of the kingdom as told to us by Mark: 'Now after John was arrested, Jesus came to Galilee, proclaiming the good news of God, and saying, "The time is fulfilled, and the kingdom of God has come near; repent, and believe in the good news"' (Mark 1:14–15).

In the space of one sentence, all of these questions are addressed and each is given a double answer. There are two indicators of time: it is after John's arrest and Jesus says that the 'appointed time' has arrived. There are also two indicators of place: the events happen in Galilee and Jesus says that the kingdom has come near. There are two indicators of what this kingdom is like: twice Jesus says that it is good news. Again, there are two indicators of how to receive the kingdom or participate in it: repent (literally turn or have a change of heart) and have faith that the news is good, that the facts are friendly. Finally, two people are mentioned: John and Jesus.

Here we have a sense that the bus is good, that, in order to get on the bus, people need to turn from what is bad in their lives and simply jump on board with confidence, and that the bus driver is Jesus. But it also seems clear that the bus came in first-century Palestine. Perhaps, then, we shouldn't be worrying so much about when or whether this bus is ever coming, but more about whether we might have missed it.

'Missing' is quite an important idea. You can miss a bus but you can also miss the point, or miss something obscure, inconspicuous and hidden. This is perhaps why, despite the talk we often hear of 'working for the kingdom', Jesus actually asks us to *look* for it. Here again, the notion of attentiveness that we encountered in our first readings seems to be important. In our readings this week it should become clear that when we pray 'Your kingdom come', this is not a way of geeing ourselves up to bring in the kingdom but, rather, a reminder that the calling of Christians is to see the kingdom (John 3:3), hear it (Matthew 13:19), receive it (Mark 10:15), speak it (Matthew 10:7), enter it (Mark 10:25), produce its fruit (Matthew 21:43), and finally to inherit it (Matthew 25:34).

At this time

So John summoned two of his disciples and sent them to the Lord to ask, 'Are you the one who is to come, or are we to wait for another?' When the men had come to him, they said, 'John the Baptist has sent us to you to ask, "Are you the one who is to come, or are we to wait for another?"' Jesus had just then cured many people of diseases, plagues, and evil spirits, and had given sight to many who were blind. And he answered them, 'Go and tell John what you have seen and heard: the blind receive their sight, the lame walk, the lepers are cleansed, the deaf hear, the dead are raised, the poor have good news brought to them. And blessed is anyone who takes no offence at me… I tell you, among those born of women no one is greater than John; yet the least in the kingdom of God is greater than he.'
LUKE 7:18B–23, 28

'The law and the prophets were in effect until John came; since then the good news of the kingdom of God is proclaimed, and everyone tries to enter it by force.'
LUKE 16:16

When is the kingdom of God? In first-century Palestine, the people of God were waiting and hoping. They were waiting and hoping for the establishment of God's rule on earth. Some of them would have seen this in highly political terms, as the establishment of a Jewish religious state and the expulsion of their Roman masters. Others may have had in mind something more apocalyptic, with God himself coming in judgment. This was the day of the LORD spoken of by the prophets, in which the present age would be wound up.

John the Baptist seems to have had the day of the LORD in mind as he preached and baptised people in the Jordan. John also speaks of 'one who is to come'. Like many who hoped for the coming of God's kingdom, he may have been thinking of the visions of Daniel, in which God promises to bestow his kingdom on a 'son of man' (Daniel 7:13–14, RSV) and his whole people (v. 27). John hoped for the coming of God's royal rule, ushered in by 'the one who is to come'.

John correctly identified Jesus as this one (Matthew 3:14; John 1:26, 29), but in today's reading he questions his earlier judgment. John starts to wonder whether the bus that is drawing up is the right one after all, or whether he should be waiting for one that will come along later. John's questioning is something that we noted in our Ash Wednesday reflection. We don't know the full story but it seems as if John was looking for a bus that would give a rather bracing ride, full of fire, judgment, and moral cleansing; but the one driven by Jesus turned out to be a party bus, full of healing, liberation, and morally dubious folk. John's question in the first of today's readings is sparked by Jesus' healing of the centurion's servant and the raising of the widow of Nain's son. Matthew's version of the story (Matthew 11:2–6) begins, 'When John heard… what the Messiah was doing…'

Jesus' response to John is very robust. He essentially says, 'Use your eyes, use your loaf, and don't close your heart to me.' He continues by talking about John with the greatest respect, but then he makes it clear that a completely new order—the kingdom of God—is being ushered in. John is yesterday's man and, if he is too fastidious about the state of the bus that is arriving, he is going to miss it altogether.

Today's second reading is from later in Luke's Gospel, when Jesus talks about John again (as with the first reading, there is a parallel version, in Matthew 11:12–13). Here Jesus makes it even clearer that John belongs to a previous age. He also emphasises, as he did right at the beginning of his ministry in Mark's Gospel, that the kingdom is good news. For Jesus, 'kingdom' is very closely linked with 'gospel'.

The old age is passing away; it is in its last days. The new age of the kingdom is arriving and being proclaimed. Proclamation here is about more than words: the kingdom is made manifest in Jesus' whole life and ministry. In all Jesus' preaching about the kingdom, the tone is urgent; time is running out. The bus is not on the horizon; it is slowing down as it approaches the bus stop. Some people, who have seen it for what it is and realised that the time is short, have already seized their opportunity and jumped forcibly on board. Their entry is rough, ready and desperate; and this is perhaps not surprising, because many of them are rough, ready and desperate folk: 'Jesus said to them, "Truly I tell you, the tax collectors and the prostitutes are going into the kingdom of God ahead of you"' (Matthew 21:31b).

When you are in a bad place, it is perhaps easier to recognise the kingdom for what it is (Matthew 5:3). If you don't think you've got a ticket, you may feel safer jumping on board before the official stop (Luke 19:4). When you are desperate, you will be prepared to run for a bus (Mark 5:6). What is certain is that the vast majority of those who drew near to Jesus, as he travelled around the towns and villages of Galilee and Judea, came to him in desperation (Luke 15:1–2). Those in easier circumstances, such as the rich young ruler (Matthew 19:22–24; Mark 10:22–25; Luke

18:23–25), seem to have decided to wait for the next bus in the hope that it would be more congenial.

So, Jesus' answer to John is that the time of waiting is over and the time to decide whether or not this is the right bus is *now*. They are standing poised at the threshold of the new age—the age of the kingdom of God. Jesus encourages his followers to greet it—indeed, to participate in its advance—by praying, 'Your kingdom come!'

Prayer

Lord God, give us urgency and desperate passion as we proclaim the good news of your kingdom.

Monday

In this place

He said therefore, 'What is the kingdom of God like? And to what should I compare it? It is like a mustard seed that someone took and sowed in the garden; it grew and became a tree, and the birds of the air made nests in its branches.' And again he said, 'To what should I compare the kingdom of God? It is like yeast that a woman took and mixed in with three measures of flour until all of it was leavened.'

Luke 13:18–21

Once Jesus was asked by the Pharisees when the kingdom of God was coming, and he answered, 'The kingdom of God is not coming with things that can be observed; nor will they say, "Look, here it is!" or "There it is!" For, in fact, the kingdom of God is among you.'

Luke 17:20–21

Where is the kingdom of God? Analogies shouldn't be pushed too far. In some ways it makes quite good sense to think of the kingdom of God as a bus. As we saw yesterday, this image captures the importance of timing, the dynamic nature of the kingdom and the requirement to enter it. In a very mundane way, we might say that the bus stop seems to have moved about somewhat, but could be localised to first-century Palestine.

Yet this really doesn't do justice to Jesus' teaching about the 'where' of the kingdom of God. In this respect, it is not at all like a great big doubledecker bus, a highly visible mechanical object occupying a bounded space in the world. Instead, it is something organic, largely hidden and obscure, but with potential to spread, to fill and transform the whole world.

The kingdom is like something very small, a mustard seed or a knob of yeast. It is so small and unprepossessing that one might miss or dismiss it altogether. Yet there is more to it than meets the eye. It looks simple but it is actually highly complex. Most of all, it undergoes transformation. The tiny mustard seed grows into a plant bigger than could ever have been guessed simply by looking at it. The yeast ferments to several times its original size.

Both the seed and the yeast give something to their world. The tree that grows from the seed offers its branches for birds of all kinds to come and nest in safety. The yeast disperses itself throughout the dough, changing it from a heavy inert lump into something light, fragrant and alive. The bread will itself be taken as nourishment by the woman and her family. Yet while the seed is germinating and growing in the dark earth, and the yeast is fermenting in a warm corner of the kitchen, the amazing power that is at work in them remains unseen.

This aspect of the kingdom perhaps explains why its approach was not just challenging or uncongenial but actually invisible to some. In today's second reading, the Pharisees ask Jesus when the kingdom is coming. They speak of it as a future event. Jesus then speaks of it in the present tense. There is an obvious difference of perspective between them, and Jesus simply says that the Pharisees cannot see the kingdom. At other points in the Gospels he says that this is because they are spiritually 'blind' (for example, Matthew 23; John 9: 39–41), but here he says that the kingdom is not something that can be seen in any sort of straightforward sense. It is here, it is at work, but the nature of its working means that it is hidden.

Jesus then says something remarkable. He locates the kingdom 'among you' (in Greek, *entos humōn)*. Much ink has been spilt in debates about how to translate *entos*, which can mean 'within', 'in your midst' or 'among'. Is Jesus saying that the kingdom is located in the hearts of these individual people? This seems highly unlikely, not least because he is talking to the Pharisees. Is he saying that the kingdom is there in the middle of them, and so suggesting that he himself embodies the kingdom? This is more of a possibility, but then he has just said that the kingdom cannot be observed, and he is highly visible. Or is he saying that the kingdom is distributed among them, secretly at work in unexpected ways and in unexpected people, such as Nicodemus (John 3:1)? This last is the most likely option, and that is why the word 'among' is used in most modern translations. It fits the secret working of the yeast and the mustard seed, and also of the wheat sown in the field (Matthew 13:24–30). The phase of the kingdom that Jesus is talking about is the hidden, growing phase. With his coming, the seeds have been sown; the yeast has been mixed. In that sense the kingdom has already arrived, though it is hard to see—but the harvest time has not yet come; the bread has not yet emerged fragrant from the oven. In this sense the kingdom has not yet come and is not yet seen in all its glory.

The first disciples were living at a time when the kingdom was active in all sorts of places and people and was in the process of spreading and becoming, yet largely hidden. In another yeasty saying, Jesus reassured them that it would not always be that way:

'Beware of the yeast of the Pharisees, that is, their hypocrisy. Nothing is covered up that will not be uncovered, and nothing secret that will not become known. Therefore whatever you have said in the dark will be heard in the light, and what you have whispered behind closed doors will be proclaimed from the housetops.' *(Luke 12:1b–3)*

The disciples were encouraged to look forward to this time by praying with eagerness, 'Your kingdom come!'

Prayer

Lord God, open our eyes to the presence of your kingdom among us.

Tuesday

Of this kind

Now there was a Pharisee named Nicodemus, a leader of the Jews. He came to Jesus by night and said to him, 'Rabbi, we know that you are a teacher who has come from God; for no one can do these signs that you do apart from the presence of God.' Jesus answered him, 'Very truly, I tell you, no one can see the kingdom of God without being born from above.' Nicodemus said to him, 'How can anyone be born after having grown old? Can one enter a second time into the mother's womb and be born?' Jesus answered, 'Very truly, I tell you, no one can enter the kingdom of God without being born of water and Spirit. What is born of the flesh is flesh, and what is born of the Spirit is spirit. Do not be astonished that I said to you, "You must be born from above." The wind blows where it chooses, and you hear the sound of it, but you do not know where it comes from or where it goes. So it is with everyone who is born of the Spirit.'
JOHN 3:1–8

For the kingdom of God is not food and drink but righteousness and peace and joy in the Holy Spirit.
ROMANS 14:17

What kind of thing is the kingdom of God? Yesterday I mentioned Nicodemus as an example of an unexpected person in whom the kingdom of God was at work. Like the seeds and the yeast, what was at work in him was hidden, and in today's reading we are told that he came to meet Jesus under cover of darkness.

Nicodemus has seen the kingdom made manifest in Jesus, he has used his eyes and his loaf and, despite the potential threat to his position (perhaps even to his life), he wants to open his heart to Jesus. Jesus takes Nicodemus very seriously. In the reading entitled 'In your room', we saw that Jesus encourages his followers to make time to get away and be alone. This will help them to maintain a heavenly perspective and to resist the perspective of the world. In today's reading Jesus again draws a distinction between a heavenly perspective and a worldly perspective. He talks to Nicodemus about 'being born from *above*'.

The kingdom of God is the kingdom of the LORD who lives beyond the skies, but it is now becoming visible on earth for those who have the eyes to see it. Its rules are not the rules of human politics but the rules of the LORD. The change of perspective that enables a human being to 'get' this kingdom is so radical that it is like a complete rebirth—a move into another realm. Jesus implies that Nicodemus is undergoing just this sort of rebirth; he, a Pharisee, has recognised that the kingdom has drawn near in a carpenter's son from Nazareth.

In another of the first set of readings, entitled 'Up the mountain', we considered the changes in perspective that can be achieved through climbing, and I suggested that prayer requires us to turn our attention upwards to seek a heavenly perspective. Yesterday we saw that there was a difference of perspective between Jesus and the Pharisees on the question of the time and place of the kingdom. In today's reading, Nicodemus seems to have at least caught a glimpse of the heavenly perspective, and Jesus makes the crucial point that what has prompted Nicodemus' undercover attempt to seek him out is the action of the Spirit. The rebirth, the radical perspective change that enables the kingdom to be both seen and entered, is powered by the Spirit. (Jesus also talks of being born of water: recall that his baptism was the occasion for his both gaining a new heavenly perspective and seeing the Spirit.)

The action of the Spirit in this reading seems to be primarily about opening people's eyes. This is referred to by the late John O'Donohue as 'the mind coming alive to an invisible geography'.[15] Dallas Willard reflects on Christian spirituality in a similar vein. He writes, 'Spirituality in human beings is... a relationship of our embodied selves to God that has the natural and irrepressible effect of making us alive to the Kingdom of God here and now in the material world.'[16]

So, not only is the kingdom closely connected with gospel and manifested in the life and ministry of Jesus, but its transforming nature is powered by the Spirit. The centrality of the Spirit in the kingdom and its pure goodness are also emphasised by Paul in our second reading.

The prayer 'Your kingdom come' can be understood as a request for the Spirit to be at work for good, both in the lives of those who pray and in the whole world. It is therefore interesting to note that some early manuscripts of Luke's Gospel are thought to have had a slight but perhaps significant difference in wording from the one that has come down to us today. Instead of 'Your kingdom come' these manuscripts had 'May your Holy Spirit come upon us and purify us.'[17]

The coming of the Spirit opens eyes, as in today's reading, but it also loosens tongues and transforms behaviour, as at Pentecost. Something of this can be seen in the life of Nicodemus. What was at work in him began in secret but, just as Jesus foretold in his pronouncements about the kingdom, it did not remain hidden. Later, presumably at great personal cost, Nicodemus publicly argued for a fair trial for Jesus (John 7:50–51), and after the crucifixion he came and cared tenderly for his body (19:39). What had been whispered behind closed doors was proclaimed from the housetop.

Prayer

Come, Holy Spirit.

In this way

People were bringing little children to him in order that he might touch them; and the disciples spoke sternly to them. But when Jesus saw this, he was indignant and said to them, 'Let the little children come to me; do not stop them; for it is to such as these that the kingdom of God belongs. Truly I tell you, whoever does not receive the kingdom of God as a little child will never enter it.' And he took them up in his arms, laid his hands on them, and blessed them.

As he was setting out on a journey, a man ran up and knelt before him, and asked him, 'Good Teacher, what must I do to inherit eternal life?' Jesus said to him, 'Why do you call me good? No one is good but God alone. You know the commandments: "You shall not murder; You shall not commit adultery; You shall not steal; You shall not bear false witness; You shall not defraud; Honour your father and mother."' He said to him, 'Teacher, I have kept all these since my youth.' Jesus, looking at him, loved him and said, 'You lack one thing; go, sell what you own, and give the money to the poor, and you will have treasure in heaven; then come, follow me.' When he heard this, he was shocked and went away grieving, for he had many possessions. Then Jesus looked around and said to his disciples, 'How hard it will be for those who have wealth to enter the kingdom of God!'

Mark 10:13–23

'The kingdom of heaven is like treasure hidden in a field, which someone found and hid; then in his joy he goes and sells all that he has and buys that field. Again, the kingdom of heaven is like

a merchant in search of fine pearls; on finding one pearl of great value, he went and sold all that he had and bought it.'
MATTHEW 13:44–46

How does a person access the kingdom of God? Or, to return to the bus analogy, how can I get a ticket?

Again and again in his teaching, Jesus returns to the theme of babies and children. We saw this in some of last week's readings, and, in yesterday's conversation with Nicodemus about wombs and rebirth, babies were not very far away.

When I was a child, one of the things that attracted me to Jesus was the fact that he took children seriously and told adults to emulate them. This was quite at odds with my experience of all other adults in my immediate circle or in public life. The world was organised from the point of view of adults, and children were expected to fit in with the adult perspective. But Jesus turns this approach upside down. Indeed, in Mark's Gospel Jesus uses a child to illustrate his famous, if enigmatic, teaching on the last being first and the first last (Mark 9:35–37).

What does it mean to receive the kingdom as a little child? Perhaps Jesus was reminding his listeners, as he often did, that we are children of our heavenly *Abba* and can trust him to give us good things. Perhaps he had in mind the ready eagerness with which a child will receive something good, and the exuberance and joy of children. Most of all, I think, he was alluding to the lack of baggage that is carried by a small child.

This baggage takes the form of possessions and personal history. It also takes the form of ingrained habits of thinking and ways of seeing life. Young children are open-minded. They have not had enough life experience to have settled on a particular way of being in the world. They are open to a wide range of possibilities. They are uninhibited, oblivious of social convention, not realising or easily forgetting that there are some things that should not be said or done; they often 'tell it as it is'. They are impulsive and tend to inhabit the immediate moment, but are also capable of astonishing levels of singlemindedness.

If the gate is narrow (Matthew 7:14) like a needle's eye (Mark 10:25), children are sufficiently unencumbered to squeeze through it. If seeing the kingdom requires losing a worldly perspective, children have less of a worldly perspective to lose. If the kingdom is partly hidden, children love to play hide-and-seek. If a decision about which bus to board has to be made now in the present moment, children are capable of responding quickly. If the kingdom is full of joy, children will be in tune with it.

Adults, on the other hand, can have too much stuff. Their ways of thinking can blind them to the kingdom. The fact that they are comfortably settled in this world makes it hard to adopt a heavenly perspective. Their responsibilities and commitments (Matthew 8:22) cause them difficulty in making impulsive and quick decisions. Their life experiences may have convinced them that they are not good enough, not entitled to receive the kingdom; unlike the young Oliver Twist, they are afraid to hold out their hands. Above all, adults consciously accumulate possessions that both express who they are and give them a sense of security in a world where they have no parents to protect them. Letting go of our stuff can be painful.

And yet, says Jesus, letting go is both necessary and worth it, for the kingdom is a hidden treasure that far outshines any amount of material possessions. These can give us some self-respect in the hard world of adult life; they can help us manage our worry about the future and can bring pleasure. But they are pale shadows of the treasure of the kingdom, which is our inheritance from our *Abba*. Here we are offered righteousness—the realisation that we are entitled to be on his bus because he has paid for our ticket himself. Here we experience deep peace and exuberant joy. All we need to do to access his kingdom is to put down our stuff, stretch out our arms and call his name.

Prayer

Lord God, Abba, let us be free from the cares that weigh us down and the habits of thought that close our minds. So may we run, fleet of foot and light of thought, into your kingdom with joy.

Thursday

Your kingdom has come

'The hour has come for the Son of Man to be glorified. Very truly, I tell you, unless a grain of wheat falls into the earth and dies, it remains just a single grain; but if it dies, it bears much fruit... Now is the judgment of this world; now the ruler of this world will be driven out. And I, when I am lifted up from the earth, will draw all people to myself.' He said this to indicate the kind of death he was to die.

JOHN 12:23–24, 31–33

If for this life only we have hoped in Christ, we are of all people most to be pitied. But in fact Christ has been raised from the dead, the first fruits of those who have died. For since death came through a human being, the resurrection of the dead has also come through a human being; for as all die in Adam, so all will be made alive in Christ. But each in his own order: Christ the first fruits, then at his coming those who belong to Christ. Then comes the end, when he hands over the kingdom to God the Father, after he has destroyed every ruler and every authority and power. For he must reign until he has put all his enemies under his feet. The last enemy to be destroyed is death.

1 CORINTHIANS 15:19–26

We now have the beginnings of some answers to our questions about the kingdom of God. It is a dynamic transformative work of the Spirit, marked by justice, personal righteousness, peace and joy. It is so radically different from the normal human ways of thinking and doing that a shift in perspective is necessary in order to see it and access it. This new perspective is in many respects child-like, and it involves an attitude of openness of heart, mind and hands. It drew near in Jesus of Nazareth 2000 years ago. It was manifest in his life and ministry, yet there was also something about it that was secret and hidden.

The kingdom was advancing in Jesus' life. With his crucifixion and raising from the dead, it finally arrived. The kingdom has come.

The seeds and the yeast are at work in the dark but, at some point, their glorious transformative work will be revealed. Nicodemus first came to Jesus under cover of darkness but he stepped into the light during Jesus' passion and finally at his death. Jesus' ministry began quietly and with a degree of secrecy but, as he approached Jerusalem, its profile was massively raised. Jesus publicly cleansed the temple and engaged in open, energetic and hostile debate with the authorities. His very entry into Jerusalem had been provocative: riding rather than walking, and choosing a donkey—an animal with royal associations (2 Samuel 16:2; Zechariah 9:9).

The kingdom movement was gathering momentum and moving towards its climax—a climax shot through with paradox. The mighty one who stilled the storm and comforted his followers with the words 'I AM' used these same words in the garden of Gethsemane to give consent to his arrest. The all-powerful one became powerless in the hands of his captors. The one who had healed and liberated so many seemed incapable of easing his own agony on the cross of execution. The one who had rejoiced in intimacy with his *Abba* felt utterly forsaken by his God. The one who offered eternal life to the rich young ruler died.

Now the deep, secret, transformative work is revealed. The

tree grows up from the ground; the loaf rises up in the oven; the first fruits of the harvest appear; the dead man bursts from the tomb. The kingdom has come. What's more, the kingdom has been given to this man.

Today's second reading makes all this completely clear. The kingdom is fully realised in the life, death and resurrection of Jesus. This is a fully human life lived from a fully heavenly perspective. Paul sets it in stark contrast to the life of Adam, which was lived from a worldly human perspective. We know that Jesus' life was heavenly because death had no hold over him. Adam died; Jesus rose. Adam was not aligned with God and hid in shame from him. Jesus was fully aligned with God and called out to him, even in his agony on the cross of shame.

Because Jesus of Nazareth was a human being, there is hope for us all. The apparent meaninglessness and extreme degree of Jesus' suffering offer particular hope to those who undergo agony, abuse and isolation, for his raising shows that even the darkest of situations is not beyond the transformative reach of God. His raising also marks the dawning of the new age and shows that, ultimately, a good harvest will come. What happened to him can happen to us too, in so far as we align ourselves with him, identify with him and remain attached to him, like the branches to the vine. Our present experience is a foretaste of our promised future inheritance— the transformation of darkness to light and death to life.

When God acted in Jesus, his kingdom was established. So does it make any sense for us to pray 'Your kingdom come' 2000 years after the event? It seems to make very little sense, and, if we look at the New Testament, we find that while Jesus talked a lot about the imminent coming of the kingdom, after his death and resurrection it is rarely mentioned by his followers, and then always as a present reality, not a future promise.

On the other hand, down the centuries Christians have honoured the words given to them by Jesus in his prayer.[18] Nevertheless, after the death and raising of Christ, these words need to be seen in a new light and spoken with a new meaning: 'By your Spirit, open our eyes to the reality of your kingdom in this world' or 'By your Spirit, help us to live in accordance with your kingdom' or 'By your Spirit, may we receive our kingdom inheritance with joy.'

Prayer

Lord Jesus, in you the kingdom was made manifest and has been fulfilled. Give us the vision and grace to live as kingdom people. In your name we pray.

Friday

The hope to which he has called you

I pray that the God of our Lord Jesus Christ, the Father of glory, may give you a spirit of wisdom and revelation as you come to know him, so that, with the eyes of your heart enlightened, you may know what is the hope to which he has called you, what are the riches of his glorious inheritance among the saints, and what is the immeasurable greatness of his power for us who believe, according to the working of his great power. God put this power to work in Christ when he raised him from the dead and seated him at his right hand in the heavenly places, far above all rule and authority and power and dominion, and above every name that is named, not only in this age but also in the age to come. And he has put all things under his feet and has made him the head over all things for the church, which is his body, the fullness of him who fills all in all.

EPHESIANS 1:17–23

When God acted in Jesus, his kingdom was established, yet it seems that, in order to see this, we need 'a spirit of wisdom and revelation'. We need to grasp the fact that Jesus really was raised and that we can know him now through his Spirit. As we get to know Christ, we will become alert to the signs of the kingdom—signs of transformation—in our world. We will see things as they really are here and now, and we will be given a vision for the future. The kingdom has come but the implications of this momentous fact have not yet reached completion.

God's action in the life, death and resurrection of Jesus was a unique cosmic event. It changed everything. The New Testament talks about it as a kind of seismic shift. Using the language of time, it speaks of a shift from a previous age into a new age. Using the language of space, it speaks of heaven breaking in to earth. Using the language of politics, it speaks of the fall of earthly regimes of power and the establishment of a new world order that is in accordance with God's will.

In last Thursday's reflection I remarked on the important place that the song of Zechariah (Luke 1:68–79) has in the worship of the church because, by reminding us of God's mighty work in Jesus, it gives us hope. Today's reading from Ephesians makes this even more explicit. We are reminded of what God has done in Jesus and told to focus on it and to hope. Hope is not some sort of bonus in the Christian life: it is our calling.

We are reminded that *Jesus* is Lord both of this age (which is passing away) and the new age that has been heralded by his coming; we are reminded that *Jesus* has passed from this earth into the heavens; and we are told in no uncertain terms that *Jesus* is Lord of a new world order that is in accordance with God's will. Our attention is redirected from questions of 'When? Where? What? and How?' to 'Who?' It is all about Jesus Christ.

The image of Christ's Lordship that is used here is not the ruler of a kingdom, but the head of a body. That body is the community of his faithful followers—the *ekklēsia* (here translated 'church'). This imagery of head and body signifies an organic interconnectedness between the risen Christ and his followers, something we have already considered in some depth in earlier readings. Christ reigns on high but his Spirit has been sent to comfort his followers, to open our eyes, to inhabit us and to transform us into his likeness. We are Christ's body on this earth. This is what Saul realised as he heard the words, 'I am Jesus, whom you are persecuting.'

One way of making sense of all of this is to return to the parable of the mustard seed. The planting of the seed, and its death in order to germinate, can be understood as the death of Jesus. The pushing of the shoot upwards, breaking the surface of the soil and becoming clearly visible as a great and growing plant, can be understood as the raising of Jesus. The growth of the tree to full maturity, with its many branches stretched out, can be understood as the flourishing of Christ's body, his people. The branches spread out into the world, offering a safe and welcoming place for all who encounter them. The tree stands tall as a beacon of hope. The hope is our hope and it is hope for the whole world. We are called to hope and we are called to share hope.

Hope and transformation are very closely linked. Television programmes that specialise in the transformation of people's drab homes, gardens or personal appearance are popular because they give a vision that things can be different—indeed, better. As followers of Christ, we are called to live transformed lives—lives that show that things can be different. Sometimes this means being 'salt of the earth', quietly giving hope at the grass roots. Sometimes it means being the 'light of the world', standing up in the public arena and challenging the status quo. It will always mean being fully present in the world, as is Christ whose fullness fills all in all.

The kingdom has come. We look forward to receiving its full inheritance as we grow up into Christ. We also look forward to something else—the coming of Christ, the Son of Man—but that is the subject of tomorrow's readings.

Prayer

Jesus is Lord!

Saturday

Marana tha!

John to the seven churches that are in Asia: Grace to you and peace from him who is and who was and who is to come, and from the seven spirits who are before his throne, and from Jesus Christ, the faithful witness, the firstborn of the dead, and the ruler of the kings of the earth. To him who loves us and freed us from our sins by his blood, and made us to be a kingdom, priests serving his God and Father, to him be glory and dominion for ever and ever. Amen.

Look! He is coming with the clouds; every eye will see him, even those who pierced him; and on his account all the tribes of the earth will wail. So it is to be. Amen. 'I am the Alpha and the Omega,' says the Lord God, who is and who was and who is to come, the Almighty…

Then I saw a new heaven and a new earth; for the first heaven and the first earth had passed away, and the sea was no more. And I saw the holy city, the new Jerusalem, coming down out of heaven from God, prepared as a bride adorned for her husband. And I heard a loud voice from the throne saying, 'See, the home of God is among mortals. He will dwell with them; they will be his peoples, and God himself will be with them; he will wipe every tear from their eyes. Death will be no more; mourning and crying and pain will be no more, for the first things have passed away.' … The one who testifies to these things says, 'Surely I am coming soon.' Amen. Come, Lord Jesus!

REVELATION 1:4–8; 21:1–4; 22:20

We do not need to wait for the kingdom or work for the kingdom. We need to look for it, receive, enter and participate in it, proclaim it, show forth its fruit and enjoy it as our inheritance for this age and the age to come. In today's reading from Revelation we find something even more amazing: *we* are that kingdom. Just as we are the body of which Christ is the head, the temple of which Christ is the cornerstone (1 Peter 2:4–7), it turns out that we are also the kingdom of which Christ is the ruler.

But still we wait. We await the time when earth is completely aligned with heaven (Romans 8:19–23), when we receive our full inheritance as children of our *Abba*, and when earthly suffering and destruction are no more. Above all, 'we would see Jesus' (John 12:21, KJV): we await, with eager anticipation, the promised coming of our Lord at the end of the age.

The very first Christians, bereaved people that they were, must have longed to see Jesus again. The rest of us long to see him for the first time, face to face. Even Paul, who had such a vivid sense of Christ's tender love for him here and now (Galatians 2:20; Philippians 3:12), still longed to see him at his coming. He writes movingly of this in his first letter to the Corinthians: 'For now we see in a mirror, dimly, but then we will see face to face. Now I know only in part; then I will know fully, even as I have been fully known' (1 Corinthians 13:12).

Paul finishes his letter with the ancient cry of the first Aramaic-speaking Christians: '*Marana tha*'. This is the same 'Our Lord, come!' that ends today's reading. Now, 2000 years after our Lord's first coming, when we pray 'Your kingdom come', this is perhaps what is deep in our hearts.

Prayer

Father, may your name be held holy. Our Lord, come!

Week 4

GIVE US EACH DAY OUR DAILY BREAD

The kingdom of God is like yeast. As we saw earlier, 'The yeast disperses itself throughout the dough, changing it from a heavy inert lump into something light, fragrant and alive. The bread will itself be taken as nourishment by the woman and her family... The loaf rises up in the oven... the dead man bursts from the tomb. The kingdom has come.'

If there is one image that is central to the Christian gospel, it is bread. In Luke's Gospel the kingdom of God is described as a place of feasting where bread is enjoyed: 'Blessed is anyone who will eat bread in the kingdom of God!' (Luke 14:15b).

Bread stands for nourishment. The daily fare of people all over the world consists of carbohydrate, supplemented to varying degrees by protein, fruit and vegetables when available. In any place where human beings have formed sizable settlements, they have cultivated a source of carbohydrate. In much of the world, it is grain for bread; in many parts of Asia, it is rice; in parts of the Americas, it is tuberous vegetables. Where people have regular access to their staple carbohydrate, they know they will not starve. They have a deep sense of security.

What we are offered in Christ is a sense of security that is like this and more. This sense of security is connected with the sense of being loved and cared for by our *Abba*, for, if our heavenly Father loves us, he will also provide for us. The image of Christ our big brother, who looks out for us (which we explored in Week 1), also gives us this sense of provision and protection. We might think of the Father as the source of bread, and the victorious risen Christ as the great breadwinner. Our hallowed heavenly Father, the kingdom and the risen Christ are all expressed in various ways through the physical substance and symbolic significance of bread.

In and through Christ, we are offered a means of satisfying all our hungers. Physical hunger is a sign of a physiological need for fuel to power our metabolism and support our body, but we have needs beyond the security and satisfaction of a full belly, and Christ satisfies these needs also. The psychologist Abraham Maslow (1908–70) is justly famous for his 'hierarchy of human needs',[19] an orderly scheme setting out the things that seem to be necessary for human flourishing. First come physiological needs that include the need for immediate nourishment; then come longer-term survival needs that include secure access to a reliable source of nourishment; then immediate relationship needs for intimacy and love; and finally comes a group of wider psycho-social needs.

There are many ways of thinking about this final group of needs. One of the most helpful has been suggested by Roy Baumeister, who describes them as 'existential needs'—that is, needs for *meaning*.[20] He proposes that, if human beings are to flourish, four basic needs for meaning must be met.

These needs are firstly 'purpose' (the need to see that our lives have a plan and a goal); secondly 'efficacy' (the need to feel competent and to make a difference); thirdly 'self-worth' (the need to feel worthy of the love and respect of others); and fourthly 'value' (the need to know that we have done and are doing the right thing in our lives). People become damaged and 'lost' when they have been deprived of purpose, efficacy, self-worth or value. Their lives will be chaotic; they will feel victims of events with no means of managing them; they will feel undeserving of love or approval; they will think that their way of life is of no value or positively shameful. In lives like these, there is a sense of alienation and lost human dignity.

Many of the human beings who encountered Jesus and whose lives were transformed by him were damaged, alienated and lost in these ways. Think of the demonised man of Gerasa (Mark 5:1–20), the woman with the haemorrhages (vv. 25–34), the man at the Sheep Gate pool (John 5:2–9), and the woman who anointed Jesus with perfume (Luke 7:37–48). Above all, think of Zacchaeus (Luke 19:1–10) and recall that, after Jesus has eaten bread with Zacchaeus he says, 'The Son of Man came to seek out and to save the lost' (v. 10). Being lost, needing to be saved, is like being hungry for good bread.

In this week's readings we will begin to explore some of the many meanings of bread, but bread is so rich a symbol that we will only be able to scratch the surface—or the crust. We need to focus on the way that Jesus uses bread in his prayer. When we do this, we will see that not just bread but *our daily* bread is important. What is 'daily' bread, and who is it for?

What's for tea?

And he said to them, 'Suppose one of you has a friend, and you go to him at midnight and say to him, "Friend, lend me three loaves of bread; for a friend of mine has arrived, and I have nothing to set before him." And he answers from within, "Do not bother me; the door has already been locked, and my children are with me in bed; I cannot get up and give you anything." I tell you, even though he will not get up and give him anything because he is his friend, at least because of his persistence he will get up and give him whatever he needs. So I say to you, Ask, and it will be given to you; search, and you will find; knock, and the door will be opened for you.'
LUKE 11:5–9

'Ask, and it will be given you; search, and you will find; knock, and the door will be opened for you. For everyone who asks receives, and everyone who searches finds, and for everyone who knocks, the door will be opened. Is there anyone among you who, if your child asks for bread, will give a stone? Or if the child asks for a fish, will give a snake? If you then, who are evil, know how to give good gifts to your children, how much more will your Father in heaven give good things to those who ask him!'
MATTHEW 7:7–11

'The Son of Man came to seek out and to save the lost'—to restore human dignity. One way in which Jesus raises human beings to a high dignity is by using human behaviour as a picture of divine behaviour. In the teaching of Jesus, frail human beings, whose motives are not always pure, are compared with the LORD, whose ways are so different from ours that they are beyond our comprehension. Yet in some mysterious and wonderful way, in the Word made flesh, the fact that human beings were created in the image of God is reclaimed and becomes apparent.[21]

Today's first reading, from Luke's Gospel, follows immediately on from the giving of the Lord's Prayer. Like the second reading, from Matthew's Gospel, it urges us to be persistent both in asking and in seeking. In both readings, the person is asking for and seeking bread. In the first reading, an adult is asking his friend to lend him food so that he can show hospitality to another friend. In the second reading, a child is asking her parent for bread, presumably because she is hungry.

We need to be alert to the types of relationships portrayed here. They are ordinary yet intimate relationships. They are also relationships within which it is reasonable to expect that one's request will be granted. Friends can be expected to do each other favours. Parents can be expected to give their children staple food. This is Jesus' model for human prayers of intercession directed at God.

However, in the history of the church we have sometimes lost sight of this model of intercessory prayer. We speak of 'petitions', a term that has its origin in absolute monarchies and empires—feudal societies in which a serf might make a request from his master, or liege lord, or the monarch, or the emperor himself (Acts 25:11). These requests were not made in the context of an intimate relationship, and there would be no expectation that the request would be granted. Much would depend on the kindness, mercy or whim of the one who held the power.

This is not how Jesus asks us to think about praying for

our daily bread. The structure of the Lord's Prayer makes it clear that our request flows firstly out of our love-bond relationship with the one he called 'Abba', so we should always expect the answer 'yes'. Secondly, it flows from a position of alignment with his kingdom values—a life lived as salt of the earth and light of the world. This is perhaps why Jesus talks of seeking as well as asking. We need to seek the right perspective in order to ask aright. When we pray for bread, we are not making a 'petition'. We are participating in a relationship where we are in tune with our Father and his mission in the world, and we are asking him to release the resources to enable that mission to be successful. This is quite a pragmatic request: 'Please can you pass over the stuff we need to be salt and light, as you have asked us to be.'

In the reading from Matthew's Gospel, children make an appearance yet again. Those of us who are parents will know the compelling, heart-melting experience of seeing a small child hold out his hand in trusting expectation of receiving good food. I well recall my children running to the kitchen door, holding their hands out for orange segments or grapes when they were toddlers. Later, as gangly teenagers, they would come crashing through the back door, dump their schoolbags down in the middle of the floor and exclaim, 'What's for tea? I'm starving!' The unspoken deal was that if I expected them to grow up, I would have to feed them. This, says Jesus, is the deal that God offers us: he wants us to grow and he will provide us with the resources to do so.

My children have long since left home. It is tidier and more peaceful without them, but I sorely miss the cry, 'What's for tea?' and even more I miss my answering, 'Tea's ready—come and get it!' So it is for God. Perhaps the universe would be tidier and more peaceful if it were not cluttered up by human beings, but God delights in us, created in his image, and he delights in responding to our cry for bread.

Prayer

Abba, we are hungry. Please give us bread.

Monday

Sufficient for the day

'Therefore I tell you, do not be anxious about your life, what you shall eat or what you shall drink, nor about your body, what you shall put on. Is not life more than food, and the body more than clothing? Look at the birds of the air: they neither sow nor reap nor gather into barns, and yet your heavenly Father feeds them. Are you not of more value than they? And which of you by being anxious can add one cubit to his span of life? And why are you anxious about clothing? Consider the lilies of the field, how they grow; they neither toil nor spin; yet I tell you, even Solomon in all his glory was not arrayed like one of these. But if God so clothes the grass of the field, which today is alive and tomorrow is thrown into the oven, will he not much more clothe you, O men of little faith? Therefore do not be anxious, saying, "What shall we eat?" or "What shall we drink?" or "What shall we wear?" For the Gentiles seek all these things; and your heavenly Father knows that you need them all. But seek first his kingdom and his righteousness, and all these things shall be yours as well. Therefore do not be anxious about tomorrow, for tomorrow will be anxious for itself. Let the day's own trouble be sufficient for the day.'
Matthew 6:25–34 (RSV)

Yesterday I was a guest at my sister's wedding. In an odd conjunction of timing, I had been meditating on today's reading while the bridesmaids were getting dressed in another part of the house. Later, as I sat in the church, I heard it read. During the reception I asked my sister why she had chosen this particular reading, and she replied, 'In the midst of all the turmoil of planning for a wedding and setting up home, I just felt the need to remember what is really important in life.' I thought that was a good answer.

Several times in the teaching of Jesus, we have a command not to 'worry'. In the Greek, the word used is *merimnaō*. It's the word that Jesus uses when he criticises Martha for being distracted by her many tasks (Luke 10:40), something we considered right at the beginning of this book. The problem with the sort of excessive concern of which Jesus speaks is that it distracts us from attentiveness to God's mission— from aligning ourselves with his perspective, looking at the birds, considering the lilies, and seeking his kingdom.

It is natural for us to want to plan ahead. Indeed, according to Roy Baumeister, human beings like to know that there is a plan, and we feel more in control of events if we can plan in advance. We need to be able to think through problems and rehearse a range of possible solutions. We need to be able to anticipate disasters in order to avoid them. This is all good, and life would soon become very dangerous and chaotic if we did not do it. Often, though, functional concern can turn into anxious preoccupation. I have sometimes referred to this sort of excessive worry as 'What-if-itis': 'What if it all goes horribly wrong? What if I don't get it all done? What if I fail? What if I am humiliated?' All this what-iffing takes up mental energy and time; our focus on future possibilities diverts us from living in and appreciating the moment, and it can make us incapable of taking any action at all. What begins as detached mental consideration can easily escalate into compulsive emotional undergoing that robs us of sleep and makes us sick at heart.

Jesus' aversion to this sort of excessive worry is summed up in a phrase that has come down to us in English as 'daily bread'. The Greek word on which this phrase is based, used by both Matthew and Luke, is *epiousios*. Ironically, this little word has caused great worry to scholars down the ages. There is nothing like it in other literature of the time. If you look up *epiousios* in a Greek dictionary, it says 'of doubtful meaning'. Because it is a unique word, some of the early church fathers thought that it must refer to the consecrated bread of Holy Communion, and this led to the promotion of the practice of taking Communion every day in some parts of the church. Others have thought it might refer to bread that will be eaten with Christ at his second coming at the end of the age.

However, the current consensus, based on careful research, is more mundane: the most likely meaning of the word is 'tomorrow's'. This would mean that we are expected to ask for enough to get us through the next 24 hours, the next three square meals: 'Give us each day our tomorrow's bread.' This prayer is, then, in solidarity with the poorest people of the world, who hire themselves out on a daily basis (Matthew 20:1–2). It is also the attitude of the young person who asks, 'What's for tea [today]?' This is a prayer that must be offered daily. However much we might want to, we can't 'front-load'; we must come continually and regularly to our *Abba* in prayer. Asking in this way expresses an extreme degree of trust that, as Jesus remarks, requires a good deal of faith. But notice that this trust is based on something—our value in God's sight. Jesus invites us to ask on the basis that we are of value. So, by asking in this way we are expressing not infantile dependency but an aspect of human flourishing— the assurance that in God's eyes we 'are worth more than many sparrows' (Matthew 10:31, NJB).

Prayer

Lord, you have told us how much we mean to you. Help us to believe your words, and give us today tomorrow's bread.

Tuesday

Travelling light

Then Jesus called the twelve together and gave them power and authority over all demons and to cure diseases, and he sent them out to proclaim the kingdom of God and to heal. He said to them, 'Take nothing for your journey, no staff, nor bag, nor bread, nor money—not even an extra tunic. Whatever house you enter, stay there, and leave from there.'
LUKE 9:1–4

Then he said to them, 'Watch, and be on your guard against avarice of any kind, for life does not consist in possessions, even when someone has more than he needs.' Then he told them a parable, 'There was once a rich man who, having had a good harvest from his land, thought to himself, "What am I to do? I have not enough room to store my crops." Then he said, "This is what I will do: I will pull down my barns and build bigger ones, and store all my grain and my goods in them, and I will say to my soul: My soul, you have plenty of good things laid by for many years to come; take things easy, eat, drink, have a good time." But God said to him, "Fool! This very night the demand will be made for your soul; and this hoard of yours, whose will it be then?" So it is when someone stores up treasure for himself instead of becoming rich in the sight of God.'
LUKE 12:15–21 (NJB)

Last week we considered the story of the rich young ruler and Jesus' teaching that too much stuff can stop us receiving or entering the kingdom. We saw that, in this context, children have an advantage over adults: they tend to have less stuff.

In today's readings, which are both from Luke's Gospel, we return to this theme, which is so important in the teaching of Jesus. In the first reading Jesus sends out the Twelve on a mission, and he exhorts them to travel light—not even to take a packed lunch. The Twelve are being sent out to proclaim and live the kingdom, and travelling light seems to be as much a part of it as teaching, healing and casting out demons. These disciples are living hand to mouth. They do not know where their next meal is coming from, never mind their bread for tomorrow.

The Twelve are sent to villages where they are to expect hospitality. This was also Jesus' practice. During his Galilean ministry he probably had a base in Capernaum but went out on extended journeys where he was completely dependent on the hospitality of others. In a previous book I have reflected on the nature of this pattern of ministry:

It gives you no conventional security whatsoever, no comfort of the familiar, no certain knowledge of where the next meal will come from, nor what the response to your message will be. There can be no confidence and authority based on being known, invited, or introduced. You are constantly a stranger. Each day is like the first day at school all over again. Perhaps that is why Jesus is so often reported as reminding his followers not to be anxious or afraid.[22]

This living on the edge fits in well with the period of Jesus' earthly life, where there was a sense of being poised at the intersection of radically different realms of time, space, and political order. It was an edgy period.

Yet it is important for us, in our apparently more settled

time, to connect with this edginess if we are to avoid complacency and live authentic Christian lives that are aligned with the kingdom. In order to enter the kingdom, we need to get rid of stuff, but then we have to keep on travelling light. Otherwise we would be like someone who goes on a diet to squeeze into a special outfit but later reverts to bad eating habits. One way of continuing to travel light is to pray and live out a daily turning to God as the source and provider of our sustenance and security—to embrace the attitude of 'give us today tomorrow's bread'.

We need to sit lightly to material goods, worldly approval and success, and we need to resist the temptation to store them up as a sort of personal insurance against our physical and existential annihilation. One might think that poor or humble people would be particularly susceptible to this sort of temptation, but instead it is wealthy and ambitious people who seem to be prone to it. The more wealth you have, the more you think you need. The more worldly recognition you have, the more afraid you become of losing it. This paradox is something that Jesus points out when he draws attention to the poor widow in the temple (Mark 12:44; Luke 21:4) and when he asserts that those who are 'poor in spirit' are the inheritors of the kingdom (Matthew 5:3).

In the second of today's readings Jesus describes a man who has much but wants to hoard more for himself. This man is anxious. He is perhaps anxious about his physical survival, but the fact that he enters into dialogue with his own soul or 'self' seems to indicate that his main worry is about his identity. He is trying to ensure his psychological survival as an individual. There is no reference to anyone else at all. He is totally concerned with himself.

There is nothing edgy here, for the man has surrounded

himself with buffers against external impact. He is a front-loader. He will not need to ask for 'tomorrow's bread' because he has bread for years to come. He sits back, a definitive picture of complacency.

The story finishes with consummate irony. We might perhaps expect thieves or fire to destroy the man's storehouses or break his body, but instead it is the man's soul—the very thing he has been trying to protect—that is demanded of him. In seeking to save his soul,[23] he has in fact lost it.

Prayer

Lord, help us to inhabit the edge, sitting lightly to the securities of this world; and give us today tomorrow's bread.

Wednesday

Bread of heaven

Then the LORD said to Moses, 'I am going to rain bread from heaven for you, and each day the people shall go out and gather enough for that day. In that way I will test them, whether they will follow my instruction or not.' …

The LORD spoke to Moses and said, 'I have heard the complaining of the Israelites; say to them, "At twilight you shall eat meat, and in the morning you shall have your fill of bread; then you shall know that I am the LORD your God."' In the evening quails came up and covered the camp; and in the morning there was a layer of dew around the camp. When the layer of dew lifted, there on the surface of the wilderness was a fine flaky substance, as fine as frost on the ground. When the Israelites saw it, they said to one another, 'What is it?' For they did not know what it was. Moses said to them, 'It is the bread that the LORD has given you to eat. This is what the LORD has commanded: "Gather as much of it as each of you needs, an omer to a person according to the number of persons, all providing for those in their own tents."' The Israelites did so, some gathering more, some less. But when they measured it with an omer, those who gathered much had nothing over, and those who gathered little had no shortage; they gathered as much as each of them needed. And Moses said to them, 'Let no one leave any of it over until morning.' But they did not listen to Moses; some left part of it until morning, and it bred worms and became foul. And Moses was angry with them. Morning by morning they gathered it, as much as each needed; but when the sun grew hot, it melted.

EXODUS 16:4, 11–21

The rich man in yesterday's reading was an individualist *par excellence*. In his short monologue, the word 'I' occurs five times and the word 'my' occurs six times. Nowhere is there a 'we' or an 'our', and the only 'you' is addressed to himself.

In contrast, the Lord's Prayer is corporate. We do not go to our rooms or up a mountain to pray, 'Give me today my daily bread.' Even when we are alone, free from the distractions of the world, we pray in solidarity with others.

Jesus' instruction to ask only for enough bread for the next 24 hours clearly stands in the tradition of today's reading, the story of the Lord's giving of manna to his people in the wilderness. Here we see that God not only wants people to trust him by gathering just what is necessary for one day; he also wants them to take into account the needs of the whole community.

There seems to be a very strong human instinct, driven by a mix of anxiety and greed, to front-load. We see it in the panic buying that takes place when there are rumours that the supermarkets are about to run short of particular goods or when an interruption in the supply of petrol is looming. This instinct must have been behind the futile attempts by some of the Israelites to gather excess manna or store it overnight.

The heavenly perspective is at complete odds with this worldly human instinct: the Lord required that the people be content with sufficient for the day, and that they be content with their fair share within the community. It becomes clear that hoarding stuff is bad not only because it gets in the way of our relationship with God, preventing an individual from entering or receiving his kingdom, but also because of the impact it has on other people, skewing the whole community so that it is out of alignment with the kingdom.

In praying for 'our' bread, we are acknowledging our interrelatedness with others. In praying for 'our daily' bread, we are acknowledging that the needs of others are equal to our own. We are committing ourselves to work for social justice as an aspect of our participation in God's kingdom. We are embracing the fact that, as Jesus said when John asked him if the kingdom had really drawn near, 'the poor have good news brought to them' (Matthew 11:5; Luke 7:22). The coming of God's kingdom means more bread for the poor and a consequent levelling of social inequalities: 'He has filled the hungry with good things, and sent the rich away empty' (Luke 1:53).

Some might wonder how far this commitment to social justice should extend. After all, in today's reading the LORD provided manna specifically for his people, the Israelites. Are we, then, simply required to work for just practices and fair distribution within Christian communities and keep out of anything that looks like secular politics? Jesus' story of the good Samaritan (Luke 10:30–37) strongly suggests that the scope of our obligation extends beyond our immediate group, to those who are unlike us. In the remainder of this week's readings we will see this theme confirmed and developed in his attitude to the sharing of bread. Jesus begins with his own people but then he broadens his horizons.

Prayer

Lord, turn our hearts outwards to see the needs of our brothers and sisters, and give us all, today, tomorrow's bread.

Thursday

The bread of life

Now when Jesus heard [that John the Baptist was dead], he withdrew from there in a boat to a deserted place by himself. But when the crowds heard it, they followed him on foot from the towns. When he went ashore, he saw a great crowd; and he had compassion for them and cured their sick. When it was evening, the disciples came to him and said, 'This is a deserted place, and the hour is now late; send the crowds away so that they may go into the villages and buy food for themselves.' Jesus said to them, 'They need not go away; you give them something to eat.' They replied, 'We have nothing here but five loaves and two fish.' And he said, 'Bring them here to me.' Then he ordered the crowds to sit down on the grass. Taking the five loaves and the two fish, he looked up to heaven, and blessed and broke the loaves, and gave them to the disciples, and the disciples gave them to the crowds. And all ate and were filled; and they took up what was left over of the broken pieces, twelve baskets full. And those who ate were about five thousand men, besides women and children.

MATTHEW 14:13–21

John the Baptist has died and the new age of the kingdom is dawning. Jesus withdraws, as is his habit when he needs head-space, to a lonely place. But by the time he gets there it is no longer lonely: it is full of people, many of them desperate. Last week, we reflected on the way that desperate people will run and force their way on to a bus, and we considered Jesus' observation that desperate people were forcing their way into the approaching kingdom. Here, desperate people hurry around the lake to intercept Jesus on his way to find some peace and quiet in the presence of his *Abba*.

Jesus then does something that is deeply characteristic of him. He *sees* the crowds and, like the Samaritan who saw the injured man on the side of the road, or like the father who saw the figure of his prodigal son on the horizon, he has compassion and he acts. The feeling of compassion that seizes him is a kind of gut-wrenching empathy that quickly moves into a 'something must be done' frame of mind. He does not judge between the deserving and the undeserving; he simply meets their need for healing.

The people stay, perhaps because they start to sense that they have stumbled upon a 'green pasture' where not only will the sick among them be healed of physical disease, but the souls of them all will be nurtured and restored (Psalm 23:2–3). (Notice how both Matthew and Mark mention that the place was grassy; Mark actually says that the grass was green: Mark 6:39.) The people's instinct is good, for they are about to be fed with the bread of life.

The story of the feeding of the 5000 is unusual in that we find it in all four Gospels (Matthew 14; Mark 6; Luke 9; John 6). This suggests that it had a particular prominence in the first Christian communities and was a greatly cherished memory of Jesus' public ministry. The theme of eating bread and fish is very strongly associated with Jesus (Matthew 7:9–10; 14:19; 15:36; Mark 6:41; 8:6–7; Luke 9:16; 24:30, 42; John 6:11; 21:9), even more strongly than bread and wine.

Bread was the staple carbohydrate in the communities of Galilee, filling the belly and providing energy. Fish would have been the main source of protein needed to supplement it, necessary for building the body and supporting full health and flourishing. This story is therefore about a massive number of people—ordinary men, women and children—getting a decent square meal, not just a snack. This is the foundation of our faith: all our hungers are met in Jesus.

But there is more. We have here a detailed picture of the grace of God, for Jesus does not produce food out of nothing. He transforms rather than creates. He takes limited human resources—paltry quantities of bread and fish and a group of rather feeble followers—and changes them. He gives the passive disciples an active diaconal role and, from meagre rations, he produces vast quantities of food. Just as God graciously invites us to join with Christ in his work of praying for the world, Jesus graciously invites his disciples to join with him in his work of feeding the people, and he graciously uses food that the people have brought for his work of transformation. Human beings are honoured here by God, who raises them up to a new dignity by incorporating them into his purposes. Jesus, who has travelled to this place to be alone with his *Abba*, now lifts his eyes heavenwards, aligning himself with the divine perspective but in company with his people.

There are extremely strong connections here with the prologue to John's Gospel, which we considered on Tuesday of Week 2. God gives 'from his fullness... grace upon grace' (John 1:16). His extravagant hospitality overflows so that there are many baskets of leftovers. Jesus is like Moses, who presided over the giving of manna to the people in the wilderness, yet he is also not like him: 'The law indeed was given through Moses; grace and truth came[24] through Jesus Christ' (v. 17). The feeding of the 5000 happens after the death of John the Baptist, whose passing forms a kind of watershed: 'John testified to him and cried out, "This was he of whom I said, 'He who comes after me ranks ahead of me because he was before me"' (v. 15). The time 'until John' is over and Jesus' time has come. There is feasting in the kingdom of God, on earth as it is in heaven.

Prayer

'Blessed be God, who feeds the hungry, who raises the poor, who fills our praise.'[25]

Friday

Crumbs under the table

And Jesus went away from there and withdrew to the district of Tyre and Sidon. And behold, a Canaanite woman from that region came out and cried, 'Have mercy on me, O Lord, Son of David; my daughter is severely possessed by a demon.' But he did not answer her a word. And his disciples came and begged him, saying, 'Send her away, for she is crying after us.' He answered, 'I was sent only to the lost sheep of the house of Israel.' But she came and knelt before him, saying, 'Lord, help me.' And he answered, 'It is not fair to take the children's bread and throw it to the dogs.' She said, 'Yes, Lord, yet even the dogs eat the crumbs that fall from their masters' table.' Then Jesus answered her, 'O woman, great is your faith! Be it done for you as you desire.' And her daughter was healed instantly.

And Jesus went on from there and passed along the Sea of Galilee. And he went up on the mountain, and sat down there. And great crowds came to him, bringing with them the lame, the maimed, the blind, the dumb, and many others, and they put them at his feet, and he healed them, so that the throng wondered, when they saw the dumb speaking, the maimed whole, the lame walking, and the blind seeing; and they glorified the God of Israel.

Then Jesus called his disciples to him and said, 'I have compassion on the crowd, because they have been with me now three days, and have nothing to eat; and I am unwilling to send them away hungry, lest they faint on the way.' And the disciples said to him, 'Where are we to get bread enough in the desert to feed so great a crowd?' And Jesus said to them, 'How many loaves have you?' They said, 'Seven, and a few small fish.' And commanding the crowd to sit down on the ground, he took the seven loaves and the fish, and having given thanks he broke them and gave them to the disciples, and the disciples gave them to the crowds. And they all ate and were satisfied; and they took up seven baskets full of the broken pieces left over. Those who ate were four thousand men, besides women and children.

MATTHEW 15:21–38 (RSV)

At first glance, it appears a bit odd that Matthew and Mark include two accounts of Jesus feeding a multitude on bread and fish. Mark's Gospel is the shortest as well as the earliest and, although he is a vivid storyteller, Mark gives us relatively little information about the ministry of Jesus compared with the other three Gospel writers. Yet he includes two almost identical versions of the same story.

Matthew almost certainly knew Mark's Gospel and drew on it when writing his own. He also used a lot of additional material from other sources, so he often cut Mark's stories quite drastically when incorporating them into his own Gospel. Yet Matthew too includes two full versions of the feeding of the multitudes. In addition, both Matthew and Mark would have written by hand on papyrus scrolls of limited length, so they would not have wanted to waste a single word. They must have had a good reason for telling us about the feeding of the 4000.

The key to this reason can be found in the material that comes between the feeding of the 5000 and the feeding of the 4000. It is essentially the same in both Gospels. First, there is the account of Jesus walking on the water that we considered on Sunday of Week 2; in the aftermath of the feeding of the 5000, the disciples catch a glimpse of the cosmic scale of Jesus' identity for the first time. Then comes an angry exchange with the Pharisees and scribes, who accuse Jesus of treating the traditions of his own culture with disrespect. In response, Jesus asserts that it is not outward forms of ritual cleanness or dietary purity that are important but, rather, a person's inner morality. It is as if Jesus is stretching the boundaries of Judaism almost to breaking point. What he has said is so radical that he has to withdraw to foreign Gentile territory until the dust has settled.

Here, in the region of Tyre and Sidon, he meets a Gentile woman who needs his help. This is a deeply significant encounter. Matthew's description of the woman as a 'Canaanite' emphasises her extreme otherness:

She stands for all that lies outside and is at odds with Jesus' patriarchal culture, for all that has for centuries been avoided and hated as godless by his people, for all that they have defined themselves against. She stands for idolatry, for polytheism, for child sacrifice, for apostasy.[26]

Jesus at first seems to resist the woman's request for help, but what begins as a conflict situation involving two individuals of different gender, religion and ethnicity ends with a 'win–win' outcome. The woman's request is granted, her daughter is healed and her faith is praised; Jesus' horizons are broadened by his encounter with the faith of a foreigner. His mission, until now focused on the Jews, is seen to be extended to include foreigners, even longstanding enemies. This mission is described in terms of bread and breadcrumbs, and is worked out in healing.

Straight after this revelatory encounter, Jesus returns to Galilee, and he then heals and feeds another massive group of people. This group, slightly smaller than the previous one, is made up of foreigners, for they 'glorified the God of Israel' (v. 31). Instead of the twelve baskets of leftovers from the feeding of the 5000, which carry overtones of the twelve tribes of Israel, we have seven baskets, a perfect number which signifies the completeness of Jesus' mission. The bread that he offers is now seen to be bread for all—'to the Jew first and also to the Greek' (Romans 1:16b).

There could be no clearer indication that the 'us' on whose behalf we are to pray for 'our daily bread', for healing and wholeness of life, refers not simply to our in-group, not simply to the church, but to the whole world.

Prayer

Lord, give us your compassion for the crowds, and make us attentive to our place in your mission to satisfy the needs of the whole world—men, women and children. In your name we pray.

Saturday

The life of the world

Then Jesus said to them, 'Very truly, I tell you, it was not Moses who gave you the bread from heaven, but it is my Father who gives you the true bread from heaven. For the bread of God is that which comes down from heaven and gives life to the world.' They said to him, 'Sir, give us this bread always.' Jesus said to them, 'I am the bread of life. Whoever comes to me will never be hungry, and whoever believes in me will never be thirsty... I am the bread of life. Your ancestors ate the manna in the wilderness, and they died. This is the bread that comes down from heaven, so that one may eat of it and not die. I am the living bread that came down from heaven. Whoever eats of this bread will live for ever; and the bread that I will give for the life of the world is my flesh.'
JOHN 6:32–35, 48–51

All our hungers are satisfied in Jesus.

We need bread to fill our bellies and power our bodies. We need to know that we have access to a dependable regular source of bread if we are to feel secure and free from the need to hoard. Our relationship with our Father offered by Jesus and worked out through the Spirit gives us this and more: it meets our needs for intimacy and love and enables us to be people with a sense of purpose, efficacy, worth and value. This is life in abundance (John 10:10), and it is life that is offered not just to a select few but to the whole world.

In the last reading of this week on the theme of bread, we go deeper still. Jesus talks about bread that gives not just abundant life here and now but life that goes on for ever.

He is referring to his death and resurrection, indicating that those who attach themselves to him can be assured of life beyond the grave. His words here resonate strongly with Paul's assertion on the nature of Christian hope that formed one of our readings for Thursday of last week. They are also linked with Jesus' discourse on attachment to the true vine that we explored on Friday of Week 1.

We receive eternal life by trusting Christ, being aligned with Christ, being organically joined to Christ, being in Christ, receiving Christ and so becoming Christ. To hammer home the fact that this is a real, substantial and total identification with Christ, we are also offered the image of eating him. This was so repugnant to Jesus' first followers that its effect was that 'many of his disciples turned back and no longer went about with him' (John 6:66). But the image is merely affirming that you are what you eat, and we are called to become as Christ.

Christ was sent by the Father as bread for the life of the world. It is into that world and for its life that he sends us.

Prayer

Father, may your name be held holy; your kingdom come; give to all people each day our daily bread.

Week 5

AND FORGIVE US OUR SINS, FOR WE OURSELVES FORGIVE EACH ONE WHO IS IN DEBT TO US

We are called to become as Christ. Central to this process is the practice of forgiveness.

It is striking that only now, quite late in the Lord's Prayer, is a mention made of the fact that we have sins that require forgiveness. It follows rather than precedes expressions of intimacy, praise, welcome for the kingdom and a request for food. How different from many of our church services! The usual practice in services of Holy Communion is to have confession very near the beginning, and definitely before receiving the bread and wine.

This practice of self-examination before making Communion is important and derives from Paul's strict injunction not to receive the body of the Lord in an unworthy manner (1 Corinthians 11:27–28). The point of self-examination is for a Christian community to identify whether there are hostile factions and splits within it. The community is the body of Christ, and so for a community riven by factions to receive consecrated bread is to commit an act of hypocrisy that treats Christ's body with contempt. Members of the community need to be at peace even with those with whom they vehemently disagree, and that is why the sharing of the peace among the community during the worship is such an important practice. In order for individuals to be at peace with each other, some apologising and forgiving may need to have taken place.

However, this practice has become rather distorted over the centuries, and many Christians have inherited the idea that each individual must make confession to God for their sins and receive absolution *in order to be made worthy* to receive Communion. It's easy both to understand this idea and to believe it, because of the deep human instinct that there are no free lunches.

Indeed, there are no free lunches, but the whole point of the gospel is that, in Christ, God has paid for our lunch. All he asks us to do is to turn to him and accept it.

So why do we need to ask for our sins to be forgiven at all?

In our readings for Week 1, we considered the story of the garden of Eden, and how the things that went wrong there were made right by Jesus in the garden of Gethsemane and its aftermath. In that context, I quoted part of the following verse: 'In Christ God was reconciling the world to himself, not counting their trespasses against them, and entrusting the message of reconciliation to us' (2 Corinthians 5:19). The key word here is 'reconciling'. Because of Christ's giving of his flesh for the life of the world, sin has been dealt with (notice that both Paul here and John in yesterday's reading talk of the world, not just believers). There is no longer enmity or separation between God and humankind: we have 'peace with God' (Romans 5:1), which is why we can call him *Abba*.

This means that, unlike Adam, we do not need to hide from God in shame, but instead we can turn to him in faith. However, we are not yet perfect, and from time to time we go wrong and slip out of alignment with the kingdom, not acting in conformity with Christ. We may feel regret or full-blown guilt when this happens, and we want to be sure that the relationship is back on track, so we ask our heavenly Father for forgiveness.

Just as we daily ask our *Abba* for bread in the context of an intimate love relationship, so do we regularly ask for forgiveness. Sometimes, when my children were of primary school age, the day would start badly, with various ones of us snappy and in a bad temper. There could be tears of frustration, hurt or anger even before breakfast had been finished (and they weren't limited to the children!). Everyone regretted it but felt stuck, so I would sometimes suggest that we rewind and 'start the day again'. The process would begin with us each taking a deep breath and saying 'Good morning' in a more positive frame of mind. It worked wonders. The basic relationships were secure—nothing would change that—but the way they played out needed constant attention if we were all to flourish.

Like our request for bread, our request for forgiveness has a social dimension. It makes no sense for us to ask for God's forgiveness and then to neglect our relationships with the people around us. Indeed, because forgiveness is so characteristic of Jesus, it should, through the Spirit, naturally become characteristic of us as we become more aligned with him. Notice how Paul, in his words from 2 Corinthians quoted above, emphasises that God is reconciled with us, so we are naturally to be reconciled with each other. Forgiveness happens in the context of reconciliation and is secondary to it. We forgive sins, we cancel debts, we decide not to count trespasses, but we are reconciled to people. That is perhaps why forgiveness comes quite late in the Lord's Prayer, for the reconciliation that has occurred between God and humanity is already implicit in its first word.

Hungry for bread

Then Jesus said, 'There was a man who had two sons. The younger of them said to his father, "Father, give me the share of the property that will belong to me." So he divided his property between them. A few days later the younger son gathered all he had and travelled to a distant country, and there he squandered his property in dissolute living. When he had spent everything, a severe famine took place throughout that country, and he began to be in need. So he went and hired himself out to one of the citizens of that country, who sent him to his fields to feed the pigs. He would gladly have filled himself with the pods that the pigs were eating; and no one gave him anything. But when he came to himself he said, "How many of my father's hired hands have bread enough and to spare, but here I am dying of hunger! I will get up and go to my father, and I will say to him, 'Father, I have sinned against heaven and before you; I am no longer worthy to be called your son; treat me like one of your hired hands.'" So he set off and went to his father. But while he was still far off, his father saw him and was filled with compassion; he ran and put his arms around him and kissed him. Then the son said to him, "Father, I have sinned against heaven and before you; I am no longer worthy to be called your son." But the father said to his slaves, "Quickly, bring out a robe—the best one—and put it on him; put a ring on his finger and sandals on his feet. And get the fatted calf and kill it, and let us eat and celebrate; for this son of mine was dead and is alive again; he was lost and is found!" And they began to celebrate.'

LUKE 15:11–24

The story of the prodigal son is deservedly one of the most famous in the Bible, for it is the story of our reconciliation with God. The reconciliation is initiated and worked by the father (who stands for God), who has been on the lookout for his son (who stands for us) long before he actually appears on the horizon. Yet the son too has his part to play. He has to turn around, come to his father and accept the free lunch— the free party—that is offered.

The son is desperately hungry for bread and he is well aware that there are no free lunches, so he has brought payment with him in the form of a confession of his sins. But before he has a chance to make his confession, his father has seen him, has been seized with the compassion that was so characteristic of Jesus, and has raced to meet and embrace him on the road.

There are many, many things that could be said about this story,[27] but for our present purposes we should note just three. First of all, the son turns to his father not from high motives but from hunger. He wants bread. He gets the bread of life. Starving, he is offered a fatted calf; aspiring to a low place in his father's household, he is offered the place of honour as his son; wanting to pay his way, he is offered a free gift; dead, he is offered life. This is all about the outrageously extravagant grace of God: 'from his fullness we have all received, grace upon grace' (John 1:16).

The next thing to notice is the cost of this grace. The alienation and reconciliation between father and son are depicted in spatial terms: the son travels far away and has to turn around to come home, and the reconciliation occurs when the distance between father and son disappears in the embrace. But there is also an issue of debt, monetary and moral. The son has taken an inheritance long before it was his due,[28] and has compounded his offence by squandering the money. His planned request to be treated like a hired hand is perhaps, then, an attempt at restitution.

It seems that the father decides to write off, or forgive, the debt. But to do this is very costly for him, as is the slaughter of the calf, as is his undignified running to greet his son, and as is his embrace of the ragged filthy figure who stinks of pigs—for he is presumably a good Jew. Just as the son is nurtured and raised to a new dignity by his father's embrace, so is the father depleted, shamed and stigmatised—and, although I have not included the final part of the story in today's reading, we also know that the father receives a tongue-lashing from his older son. Here there are deep resonances with the suffering servant of Isaiah:

He was despised and rejected by men; a man of sorrows, and acquainted with grief; and as one from whom men hide their faces he was despised, and we esteemed him not. Surely he has borne our griefs and carried our sorrows; yet we esteemed him stricken, smitten by God, and afflicted. But he was wounded for our transgressions, he was bruised for our iniquities; upon him was the chastisement that made us whole, and with his stripes we are healed. (Isaiah 53:3–5, RSV)

This tongue-lashing from the older son brings us to the third point. The transaction between the father and his younger son is not private. The whole household and probably the neighbours are drawn in. The father doesn't organise a dinner for two; he throws a noisy party. And later, in response to the chastisement by his older son, he emphasises that the younger son is 'your brother' (Luke 15:32). 'Beloved, since God loved us so much, we also ought to love one another' (1 John 4:11).

Prayer

Abba, when I go wrong, help me to see it, to name it and to turn homewards to you.

Coming to tea

He entered Jericho and was going through the town and suddenly a man whose name was Zacchaeus made his appearance; he was one of the senior tax collectors and a wealthy man. He kept trying to see which Jesus was, but he was too short and could not see him for the crowd; so he ran ahead and climbed a sycamore tree to catch a glimpse of Jesus who was to pass that way. When Jesus reached the spot he looked up and spoke to him, 'Zacchaeus, come down. Hurry, because I am to stay at your house today.' And he hurried down and welcomed him joyfully. They all complained when they saw what was happening. 'He has gone to stay at a sinner's house,' they said. But Zacchaeus stood his ground and said to the Lord, 'Look, sir, I am going to give half my property to the poor, and if I have cheated anybody I will pay him back four times the amount.' And Jesus said to him, 'Today salvation has come to this house, because this man too is a son of Abraham; for the Son of man has come to seek out and save what was lost.'
Luke 19:1–10 (NJB)

The account of Jesus and Zacchaeus comes a few chapters after the story of the father and his lost son in Luke's Gospel. In many ways it can be seen as a real-life worked example of the theology in that story. It also moves on from it, showing what happens in a person's life when he realises that he is reconciled with God.

Zacchaeus has taken the wrong road in his life: indeed, Jesus describes him as 'lost'. As a tax collector on behalf of the Romans, he has 'hired himself out to a citizen of that country': in handling their money, he has dirtied himself, just as much as the lost son who cared for pigs. As with the lost son, there is dirt and there is debt. By his actions Zacchaeus has made himself *persona non grata* among his upright Jewish neighbours, and, like the lost son, he is not satisfied. Perhaps he is even desperate for something better: he climbs up a tree and tries to see Jesus.

Jesus, like the father in the story, directs his gaze at the one who is lost. He then offers a metaphorical embrace and a real feast, for, in the words of a very old Sunday school song, he invites himself to tea:

> Zacchaeus was a very little man
> and a very little man was he.
> He climbed up into a sycamore tree
> for the Saviour he wanted to see.
> And when Jesus passed that way
> he looked into the tree
> [spoken] and said, 'Now Zacchaeus, you come down,
> for I'm coming to your house for tea.'[29]

There is nothing more affirming when you are a small child than being invited to play at someone's house after school, and to stay for tea. It's a mark of friendship and of finding a place in the wider community. I recently heard this said by a parent on a television relocation show: 'He's really settled into his school. He's been to quite a few places for tea and we've had kids here for tea.'

But there's nothing so sad as a small child who never gets to go to tea or to have someone round to their place for tea. Unlike the prodigal son, Zacchaeus has enough money for food; he just doesn't have anyone who wants to eat it with him. His hunger is for love and acceptance, something he has been unable to purchase, but his hunger is met in Jesus, whom he welcomes with great joy. Then *and only then* does Zacchaeus talk of his previous fraudulent practice. This is the same order of things that we find in the Lord's Prayer: love, intimacy, a vision of the kingdom, the relief of hunger, then an acknowledgment of sin. Zacchaeus' desire to make restitution to those he has cheated flows out of the reconciliation that is initiated by and effected through Christ. Notice how Zacchaeus' dignity is raised through this encounter: the little man stands up straight when he is in the company of Jesus. Like the lost son, he 'came to himself'.

There is also here a parallel with the judgmental older brother of the prodigal son. The respectable neighbours criticise Jesus, for he has become stigmatised by his association with Zacchaeus. The cost of Zacchaeus' welcome is the tainting of Jesus. Yet, like the father in the story, Jesus insists that this is a matter that affects the whole family: 'he too is a son of Abraham'.

Jesus pays a price for the salvation of Zacchaeus (1 Corinthians 6:20), and Zacchaeus responds by giving his money to those in need. It is when we grasp what God has done for us—the generosity of the gift and what it cost him—that our lives begin to change. The 'grace upon grace' that we receive from God naturally overflows into the lives of those around us, its effects spreading like ripples in a pond. We might say that Zacchaeus responds to Jesus out of gratitude, but in tomorrow's reading, as we shall see, Jesus uses a different word: love.

Prayer

God of justice and generosity, we have received grace upon grace at your hands. How could we ever hope to repay you?

Because he first loved us

One of the Pharisees asked Jesus to eat with him, and he went into the Pharisee's house and took his place at the table. And a woman in the city, who was a sinner, having learned that he was eating in the Pharisee's house, brought an alabaster jar of ointment. She stood behind him at his feet, weeping, and began to bathe his feet with her tears and to dry them with her hair. Then she continued kissing his feet and anointing them with the ointment.

Now when the Pharisee who had invited him saw it, he said to himself, 'If this man were a prophet, he would have known who and what kind of woman this is who is touching him—that she is a sinner.' Jesus spoke up and said to him, 'Simon, I have something to say to you.' 'Teacher,' he replied, 'speak.' 'A certain creditor had two debtors; one owed five hundred denarii, and the other fifty. When they could not pay, he cancelled the debts for both of them. Now which of them will love him more?' Simon answered, 'I suppose the one for whom he cancelled the greater debt.' And Jesus said to him, 'You have judged rightly.'

Then turning toward the woman, he said to Simon, 'Do you see this woman? I entered your house; you gave me no water for my feet, but she has bathed my feet with her tears and dried them with her hair. You gave me no kiss, but from the time I came in she has not stopped kissing my feet. You did not anoint my head with oil, but she has anointed my feet with ointment. Therefore, I tell you, her sins, which were many, have been forgiven; hence she has shown great love. But the one to whom little is forgiven, loves little.' Then he said to her, 'Your sins are forgiven.'

But those who were at the table with him began to say among

themselves, 'Who is this who even forgives sins?' And he said to the
woman, 'Your faith has saved you; go in peace.'
Luke 7:36–50

Luke's version of the forgiveness section of the Lord's Prayer differs slightly from Matthew's. Matthew 6:12 says, 'And forgive us our debts, as we also have forgiven our debtors', whereas Luke 11:4 says, 'And forgive us our sins, for we ourselves forgive everyone indebted to us.' These are really just differences of style. Both indicate that we ask for God's forgiveness in a context of forgiving others. Matthew implies that we forgive lots of times (this is even clearer in tomorrow's reading); Luke implies that we have a continuous attitude of forgiveness. Matthew uses the word 'debt' (*opheilēma*) twice; Luke uses the word 'sin' (*hamartia*) once and the word 'debt' once, as if they were interchangeable.

The concept of 'debt' has already emerged as an important theme in our previous readings this week. The wording of the Lord's Prayer makes it clear that forgiveness is about the writing off of a debt. The word that we translate 'forgive' is *aphiēmi*, which literally means to 'let (it) go'. In his version of the Lord's Prayer, Luke indicates that the sort of debt that is being 'let go' is a moral debt: our debt is let go, our sins are forgiven. We are redeemed (Ephesians 1:7).

In today's reading, again from Luke's Gospel, Jesus draws a very close connection between the forgiveness of sins and the cancellation of a debt. The woman who enters Simon's house is 'a sinner' (and Jesus says that her sins were 'many'). We are not told explicitly what kind of sins she has committed but she is described as 'this kind of woman', so there is a strong implication that she is a prostitute. This profession was the female equivalent of tax collecting, because the woman's business would have been plied among the Roman occupiers. (Recall that it is the tax collectors and prostitutes that Jesus mentions as jumping aboard the kingdom before the chief priests and elders in Matthew 21:31.)

The woman has grasped what God has done for her and she is overwhelmed with emotion. She expresses herself in the way she knows best. Zacchaeus gave money away; she offers Jesus a massage with very expensive ointment, perhaps ointment that she would have used in her trade. This is disgusting for the onlookers, for the woman taints Jesus by her touch, but notice that just as the lost son's status was raised and just as Zacchaeus stood up straight, this woman also is raised up by Jesus. He reinterprets her actions as those of a host who receives him with the joy, care, and respect that are his due, and he uses her behaviour to throw Simon's deficiencies as a host into relief. The woman has realised that she is reconciled with God through Jesus. She has pushed into the house and she has received the kingdom.

Her actions are extravagant and embarrassing but they are in proportion to her sense of the extravagant grace of God— the massive debt that he has let go. Yet her actions do not arise simply out of gratitude. She is not engaging in some sort of transaction. She has received 'grace upon grace'; she senses that she is in a love relationship and she is moved to tears. She's in love and she can't help but show it. Amazingly, Jesus recognises her emotional outpouring as saving 'faith'. It is a response to the felt love of God, a response that has something of remorse about it, as does Zacchaeus' reference to his past sins. These two are not saved by their expressions of remorse; their expressions of remorse indicate that they have been saved.

Prayer

God of justice and generosity, we have received grace upon grace at your hands. We love you so.

Kissing up and kicking down

Then Peter went up to him and said, 'Lord, how often must I forgive my brother if he wrongs me? As often as seven times?' Jesus answered, 'Not seven, I tell you, but seventy-seven times.

'And so the kingdom of Heaven may be compared to a king who decided to settle his accounts with his servants. When the reckoning began, they brought him a man who owed ten thousand talents; he had no means of paying, so his master gave orders that he should be sold, together with his wife and children and all his possessions, to meet the debt. At this, the servant threw himself down at his master's feet, with the words, "Be patient with me and I will pay the whole sum." And the servant's master felt so sorry for him that he let him go and cancelled the debt. Now as this servant went out, he happened to meet a fellow-servant who owed him one hundred denarii; and he seized him by the throat and began to throttle him, saying, "Pay what you owe me." His fellow-servant fell at his feet and appealed to him, saying, "Be patient with me and I will pay you." But the other would not agree; on the contrary, he had him thrown into prison till he should pay the debt. His fellow-servants were deeply distressed when they saw what had happened, and they went to their master and reported the whole affair to him. Then the master sent for the man and said to him, "You wicked servant, I cancelled all that debt of yours when you appealed to me. Were you not bound, then, to have pity on your fellow-servant just as I had pity on you?" And in his anger the master handed him over to the torturers till he should pay all his debt.

And that is how my heavenly Father will deal with you unless you each forgive your brother from your heart.'
MATTHEW 18:21–35 (NJB)

In today's reading, this time from Matthew's Gospel, Jesus tells a parable that again emphasises the link between forgiveness of sins and cancellation of debts. It's a vivid story that would have made a lot of sense to his hearers, for it was told in a society where whole families were regularly thrown into prison or sold into slavery for non-payment of debts. It has a resonance for our society, too. Many people are deeply troubled by money worries—credit card bills, mortgages or loans from finance companies. Some borrow money from unscrupulous loan sharks at enormous rates of interest. If they can't pay up, the bailiffs may be sent in or, worse, intimidating thugs may pay them a visit.

To know that a debt like this has been cancelled brings a sweet sense of relief and deep peace. This peace should naturally overflow to others, but sometimes it doesn't. The servant in this story, like the woman in yesterday's reading, has a 'kiss up' attitude. Sadly, he also has a 'kick down' attitude. He comes before his master, powerless, in apparent deference and humility, but he bullies one of his peers who is under his power. The servant has not grasped the generosity and mercy of his master; he merely does what he thinks is necessary to get his debt cancelled. He feels entitled to what he has gained; he does not receive it as a gift. He also feels special and different, for he is not able to make the connection that is so obvious to his fellow servants and to us: the servant whom he abuses is just like him. 'There but for the grace of God go I.'

This sort of attitude is characteristic of narcissism, a

personality trait that, in recent research, has been shown to be associated with both an unforgiving and an unrepentant approach to life. Narcissistic people think they are special, entitled to ride rough-shod over others. In this story, Jesus is reminding Peter that forgiveness is a gift, received by all: we are all equally special and we are all like each other because we have all been in debt. One of the first steps in human forgiveness is to be able to see the other person as 'like me'. So forgiveness is an aspect of solidarity.

Solidarity is delightfully evident in this story in the actions of the fellow servants who, unlike the bully, easily feel empathy for their colleague and act as his advocates. They sense that a deep injustice has taken place. The injustice concerns the abuse of power.

Forgiveness is the letting go of something to which we are entitled—an interpersonal debt. If we can see this, we will also see that forgiveness is possible only if you are a creditor who is in a position to enforce payment from your debtor; that is, it is only possible from a position of power. In this story, it would make no sense at all for the debtor to write off the debt of his creditor; the creditor doesn't owe him anything. The weak are not required to forgive the strong while they remain in a position of weakness—it simply makes no sense. People who are stuck in abusive relationships in which they have no power over their abusers are not required to forgive. This story is for us all, but it is actually told in response to a question about community order by Peter, the first pope, and it is addressed to the inner circle of the disciples, who will become the first church leaders. Leaders have a particular vulnerability to thinking that they are special and lording it over others (Matthew 20:25; Mark 10:42; Luke 22:25).

The abuse of power is something that is treated with the

greatest seriousness by the New Testament writers, and it is in this context that images of cruel punishment are invoked. Jesus' most punitive images are reserved for the rich man who ignored Lazarus at his gate (Luke 16:23) and Christian leaders who mislead or abuse those in their charge (Mark 9:42–43; Luke 12:47). We may find these images unpalatable but they remind us of God's justice, of his immense holiness and otherness, and they should help us never to take for granted the fact that we can call him *Abba*.

Prayer

God of justice and generosity, make us alert to injustice and cruelty, ready to stand in solidarity with those who are abused and oppressed and to plead their cause. This we ask in the name of our advocate, Jesus Christ the righteous.

Children of the Most High

'Whenever you stand praying, forgive, if you have anything against anyone; so that your Father in heaven may also forgive you your trespasses.'
MARK 11:25

'Do to others as you would have them do to you. If you love those who love you, what credit is that to you? For even sinners love those who love them. If you do good to those who do good to you, what credit is that to you? For even sinners do the same. If you lend to those from whom you hope to receive, what credit is that to you? Even sinners lend to sinners, to receive as much again. But love your enemies, do good, and lend, expecting nothing in return. Your reward will be great, and you will be children of the Most High; for he is kind to the ungrateful and the wicked. Be merciful, just as your Father is merciful. Do not judge, and you will not be judged; do not condemn, and you will not be condemned. Forgive, and you will be forgiven; give, and it will be given to you. A good measure, pressed down, shaken together, running over, will be put into your lap; for the measure you give will be the measure you get back.'
LUKE 6:35–38

In yesterday's reading, when Peter asks Jesus if he should forgive his brother 'as many as seven times' he is using an expression that indicates a comprehensive level of forgiveness. Recall that the feeding of the 4000 involves the number seven, which signifies completeness. So Peter is really asking if his forgiveness should be total. Jesus makes a response that is ridiculous in scale to emphasise his point—essentially saying, 'infinity times infinity'. What Jesus is getting at here and in the forgiveness section of the Lord's Prayer is the cultivation of an *attitude* of forgiveness.

An attitude is an enduring disposition towards something or someone. It is a directional sort of thing, and so relates to alignment. If we are aligned with Christ, we will have to have certain attitudes. In our readings for Week 2, we explored the idea of prayer as an 'intentional stance' (notice that today's first reading includes the words 'stand praying'). To cultivate an attitude of forgiveness is to take an intentional stance. Forgiveness is therefore closely related to prayer, and so it is not surprising that Jesus taught his followers not simply to pray for forgiveness, but to make an attitude of forgiveness part of their prayer.

In today's short first reading, we see another trace of the Lord's Prayer in Mark's Gospel. In the garden of Gethsemane, Jesus prays for his *Abba*'s will to be done and for him to be spared the coming time of trial. Here he instructs his disciples to pray with a forgiving attitude. We are reconciled with God our Father; the relationship is secure, but we are not in a position to ask for our day-to-day wrongdoings to be forgiven until we adopt a forgiving attitude to others.

The problem can be that we don't feel much like forgiving. We might like to be able to feel that way, but we don't. This isn't as much of a problem as it might seem, because the thing about an attitude is that it involves turning in a certain direction, not necessarily moving very far along the road. It's like Peter turning to Jesus and taking a few steps on the water before his weakness has to be supported by Jesus, like the lost son deciding to turn homewards but being met and accompanied by his father, or like the man who said to

Jesus, 'I believe, help my unbelief!' and whose son was then healed (Mark 9:24). We don't need to conjure up all sorts of insincere feelings of affection for someone who has hurt us (and then feel guilty when the feelings can't be sustained); we simply need to want to forgive, and offer the relationship to God.

In the second of today's readings, the attitude of forgiveness is presented as an aspect of something bigger—an attitude of love. As we saw in the context of asking for daily bread, this attitude of love should extend to all in the church community and out into the world. But what does it mean to 'love your enemies'?

Just as in the story of the good Samaritan, Jesus says here simply that we should treat members of 'out-groups' as if they were members of our 'in-group'. Human beings have a very strongly ingrained tendency to form groups that build up solidarity and connectedness. This is a natural and good thing, but the other side of the coin is a hostile attitude towards out-groups. This is what happened in Britain during World War II: the mental health of the nation was never better, for everyone had his or her place of value, working towards a common goal, but it was achieved at the cost of fear and hatred of the enemy. In an extreme form it's what happens in genocide and sectarian violence, but it is also what happens in little ways in our everyday lives all the time. The churches are, sadly, not immune; in fact, we are rather prone to it, and some of us are quite ready to divide the world into the saved and the lost. Yet this is not the way of Jesus, who told the story of the wheat and the tares (Matthew 13:24–30) and, in today's reading, instructs his followers not to judge or condemn.

In human society, the cost of in-group solidarity is out-group hostility. This is not the pattern of the kingdom, for the cost has been met by Jesus, whose non-retaliative stance towards his enemies and executioners was vindicated by his resurrection. Jesus both modelled and made possible a profound type of group solidarity that is at the same time kindly rather than hostile to outsiders, those who are different, and even those who wish us harm. It is by aligning ourselves with his stance that we are raised up to be children of God.

Prayer

Lord, we bring you our little will to forgive. Take it and transform it into a love that heals wounds, breaks down barriers and makes peace. So we shall be called the children of God.

Friday

Walking the talk

This is the message we have heard from him and proclaim to you, that God is light and in him there is no darkness at all. If we say that we have fellowship with him while we are walking in darkness, we lie and do not do what is true; but if we walk in the light as he himself is in the light, we have fellowship with one another, and the blood of Jesus his Son cleanses us from all sin. If we say that we have no sin, we deceive ourselves, and the truth is not in us. If we confess our sins, he who is faithful and just will forgive us our sins and cleanse us from all unrighteousness. If we say that we have not sinned, we make him a liar, and his word is not in us.

My little children, I am writing these things to you so that you may not sin. But if anyone does sin, we have an advocate with the Father, Jesus Christ the righteous; and he is the hilasmos[30] *for our sins, and not for ours only but also for the sins of the whole world. Now by this we may be sure that we know him, if we obey his commandments. Whoever says, 'I have come to know him', but does not obey his commandments, is a liar, and in such a person the truth does not exist; but whoever obeys his word, truly in this person the love of God has reached perfection. By this we may be sure that we are in him: whoever says, 'I abide in him', ought to walk just as he walked.*

1 John 1:5—2:6

In exploring yesterday's reading, I suggested that Jesus has met the cost of in-group solidarity, enabling and calling us to be free from out-group hostility. This is one way of understanding the way in which 'in Christ God was reconciling the world to himself'—as a kind of redemption.

In today's reading, from the first letter of John,[31] we are presented with another way of understanding the work of Christ: Jesus the *hilasmos*. This Greek word has been the subject of much controversy among translators. Its literal meaning is 'the means by which sins are forgiven', so it tells us that because of Jesus the sins of the whole world—not just our sins—are forgiven. It doesn't tell us how. Nevertheless, because John talks about Jesus' blood, there are sacrificial overtones. In Week 1 we explored the idea of Jesus' blood as life-giving and noted that the life-giving properties of blood lie behind the practice of animal sacrifices. Here, Jesus' blood is seen as cleansing (an idea that is taken up in Revelation 7:14).

Blood sacrifice is, on the surface, rather alien to our modern sensibilities, yet the symbolic power of blood goes very deep in the human psyche and, for many people, it remains a compelling image of the work of Christ. But it doesn't matter too much which image we choose (and the Bible provides us with several). The bottom line is that in and through Christ we have peace with God and forgiveness of sins.

John locates this forgiveness firmly in a relationship of fellowship with God, which naturally flows into a relationship of fellowship with each other, using images of walking in his light, of receiving his truth, and of knowing him. His language is quite frank: if you claim to know God and yet act out of alignment with his nature, you are simply a liar. This idea of lying is important because it brings us back to the significance of words, which we considered in Week 1. There we looked at the language of intimacy that we are given by the Spirit. Here we see that this language is also the language of authenticity. If we know God well and are known by God, if we are his children, we will speak the truth. That means that we will be honest about our shortcomings, coming confidently to God for forgiveness rather than denying them to ourselves and others for fear of being found out and exposed.

Finally, John talks of 'abiding in God'. This reminds us of Jesus' discourse on the true vine, and it brings us back to where this book started—the idea that our calling as Christians is to be in Christ. If we are in Christ, we will walk as he walked and we will embrace forgiveness.

In tomorrow's reading we will come full circle and look at the story of Stephen, but first I will summarise the character of Christian forgiveness that has emerged in this week's readings.

- Forgiveness flows out of our consciousness that we have been reconciled with God, and that this is a costly and generous gift, not our entitlement.
- Forgiveness is the cancellation of a consciously acknowledged interpersonal debt, not a denial that the debt exists.
- Forgiveness is an intentional stance and does not necessarily show itself in warm feelings towards the offender.
- We can only offer forgiveness from a position of strength or power. If we have no way of enforcing payment of the interpersonal debt, then we are not required to offer forgiveness. In fact, an authentic offer of forgiveness is a sign of strength and power.
- Sometimes our role is to stand in solidarity with those who are weak and abused, to stop the offence, to name the interpersonal debt and support the victim's move into a position of strength.

- It makes no sense to forgive in the midst of the offence. Forgiveness is something that happens when the offence has been completed and we have had time to reflect on it and recognise that an interpersonal debt exists.
- If we are in a position of strength and power, we are to offer forgiveness even in the absence of repentance.
- Our practice of forgiveness is a sign that we are children of God, builds up the body of Christ, and is an expression of God's love for the whole world.

Prayer

Forgive us our sins, for we ourselves forgive each one who is in debt to us.

Drinking the cup

Stephen, full of grace and power, did great wonders and signs among the people. Then some of those who belonged to the synagogue of the Freedmen (as it was called), Cyrenians, Alexandrians, and others of those from Cilicia and Asia, stood up and argued with Stephen. But they could not withstand the wisdom and the Spirit with which he spoke. Then they secretly instigated some men to say, 'We have heard him speak blasphemous words against Moses and God.' They stirred up the people as well as the elders and the scribes; then they suddenly confronted him, seized him, and brought him before the council. They set up false witnesses who said, 'This man never stops saying things against this holy place and the law; for we have heard him say that this Jesus of Nazareth will destroy this place and will change the customs that Moses handed on to us.' And all who sat in the council looked intently at him, and they saw that his face was like the face of an angel...

[Stephen said] 'Which of the prophets did your ancestors not persecute? They killed those who foretold the coming of the Righteous One, and now you have become his betrayers and murderers. You are the ones that received the law as ordained by angels, and yet you have not kept it.' When they heard these things, they became enraged and ground their teeth at Stephen. But filled with the Holy Spirit, he gazed into heaven and saw the glory of God and Jesus standing at the right hand of God. 'Look,' he said, 'I see the heavens opened and the Son of Man standing at the right hand of God!' But they covered their ears, and with a loud shout all rushed together against him. Then they dragged him out of the city and began to stone him; and the witnesses laid

their coats at the feet of a young man named Saul. While they were
stoning Stephen, he prayed, 'Lord Jesus, receive my spirit.' Then he
knelt down and cried out in a loud voice, 'Lord, do not hold this sin
against them.' When he had said this, he died.

Acts 6:8–15; 7:52–60

And so we return to Stephen. In Week 1 we considered his faith, his authentic speech in the Spirit, his heavenly perspective, and his alignment with Christ through his forgiveness of his murderers. Today we will explore the nature of this forgiveness in a little more depth.

Stephen was someone who 'walked the talk', who took up his cross (Matthew 16:24; Mark 8:34; Luke 9:23) and drank the cup (Matthew 20:22; Mark 10:38). He was one of the first deacons, taking on administrative and domestic tasks in the Jerusalem church. In his calling to be a servant of the community, he was already identifying strongly with Jesus. His servant ministry was not quiet and self-effacing: like Jesus, he performed wonders and spoke with wisdom and authority. Nor did he avoid confrontation. Forgiveness is not about avoidance of confrontation; in fact, it may require it. Like Jesus, who was both assertive and confrontational with the Pharisees, Stephen was assertive and downright inflammatory in his speech to the high priest and Sanhedrin. It's not surprising that they 'became enraged and ground their teeth'! Here we have a model of Christian ministry that is strong, courageous and prophetic.

Then a crime is committed against Stephen. He is effectively lynched. As the offence draws towards its close, Stephen names it 'this sin' and he shows himself still to be in a position of strength, for he calls upon his Lord, who has the power to condemn, and asks that the debt be written off.

That is all that is required of us—to wait until the offence is complete, to make sure that we are in a place of strength and support, to name the offence, and to ask God's help in writing it off.

Prayer

Father, may your name be held holy; your kingdom come; give us each day our daily bread, and forgive us our sins, for we ourselves forgive each one who is in debt to us.

Holy Week

AND DO NOT PUT US TO THE TEST

This is the sixth full week of readings for Lent. As we have done on the sixth day of each week, we need to pause. It is also Holy Week, when, as we follow Christ's passion, 2000 years of time seem to collapse. We need to pause, to watch, and to wait.

The readings for this week therefore simply follow the passion narrative as told to us by Luke. My feeling is that this narrative is so powerful that detailed commentary should not be allowed to stand in its way. So, for each reading, I simply make a connection with themes from the Lord's Prayer that we have encountered in our reflections through Lent. I also suggest a return to a previous reflection, indicating particular points of connection by bold type in the text of the passion narrative. Thus the Lord's Prayer can be seen in the light of the passion of Christ and the passion of Christ can be seen in the light of the Lord's Prayer. This is in the spirit of the Easter command of the angels to 'remember how he told you...' (Luke 24:6).

The final line of the Lord's Prayer, in both Matthew and Luke, includes the word *peirasmos*, which can be translated 'trial', 'temptation' or 'test'. It has the sense of a process of suffering and affliction, out of which great rewards may come but which we would rather avoid.

In my work as a clinical psychologist with people who had suffered serious injury and illness, I became interested in something called 'post-traumatic growth'. This is the paradoxical finding that, for many people, even the worst of experiences can bring gains that cannot occur in any other way. When I talked to people who had been through deep trauma and yet come out on the other side enriched, they always made it very clear that they would rather have avoided the trauma at almost any cost and wouldn't wish it on anyone else, *but*, astonishingly, there were 'treasures that can only be found in darkness' (see Isaiah 45:3).[32] There is something of this behind Jesus' struggle in the garden—its terrible nature vividly communicated by Luke. Jesus wants to avoid the cross if it is at all possible, but, with the support of an angel who helps him retain his grasp on the divine perspective, he comes to understand that this is going to be the only way and his resolve is strengthened.

What Jesus undergoes in the olive grove is a reprise of what he has undergone in his testing (*peirazomenos*) in the wilderness (and also at Caesarea Philippi). It is in the wilderness, straight after receiving words of love and assurance from his *Abba* at his baptism, that he has to struggle with what it means to be the Son of God. He must have been increasingly aware of his special powers; what's more, his heavenly Father had revealed himself to him and blessed him. The temptation then to think of himself as 'special'—the temptation to narcissism—must have been almost overwhelming.

As we saw in an earlier reading, Jesus faced three decisions in the wilderness, the first one involving bread (for it is never far away in the Gospels). He could use his special powers and status to avoid the realities of being fully human. Secondly, he could use his special powers and status to rule the world. Thirdly, he could use his special powers and status to avoid placing trust in his Father. In a recent children's presentation, I described these options as 'cheating', 'bossing people about' and 'doing his own thing'. I asked the children whether these would have been good choices, and what choices Jesus actually made. Together we worked out that Jesus didn't cheat but allowed himself to be a real human being who got hungry and thirsty and felt pain; and that instead of bossing people about he decided to use his special powers to help people (Luke 4:18–19). Then I asked the children if anyone could think of a time when Jesus had decided not to do his own thing with his special powers, but to rely on his Father instead. One little boy opened his eyes wide, shot up his hand and exclaimed in wonder, 'When he died!' He was, of course, correct.

The struggle on the Mount of Olives comes not too long after Jesus' acclamation as king as he enters Jerusalem and his poignant farewell supper with his disciples, where bread is again central. He has to set aside human power, glory and the pressure from those who want to 'make him king' (John 6:15). He also has to relinquish the companionship of dearly beloved friends. He turns and takes an intentional stance, something that Luke describes elsewhere as 'setting his face' (Luke 9:51), and allows himself to be handed over by Judas. Unlike the warm and passionate kisses of the woman with the alabaster jar (Luke 7:38), Judas' kiss is cold steel; it seems to go straight into Jesus' heart.

Through prayer, Jesus has made his monumental decision, has set his face and has taken his supremely costly intentional stance. His fate and the fate of the world are then sealed. The powers of darkness are defeated and the kingdom is round the corner: 'Now is the judgment of this world; now the ruler of this world will be driven out' (John 12:31).

Blessed is the king

After he had said this, he went on ahead, going up to Jerusalem. When he had come near Bethphage and Bethany, at the place called the Mount of Olives, he sent two of the disciples, saying, 'Go into the village ahead of you, and as you enter it you will find tied there a colt that has never been ridden. Untie it and bring it here. If anyone asks you, "Why are you untying it?" just say this: "The Lord needs it."' So those who were sent departed and found it as he had told them. As they were untying the colt, its owners asked them, 'Why are you untying the colt?' They said, 'The Lord needs it.' Then they brought it to Jesus; and after throwing their cloaks on the colt, they set Jesus on it. As he rode along, people kept spreading their cloaks on the road. As he was now approaching the path down from the Mount of Olives, the whole multitude of the disciples began to praise God joyfully with a loud voice for all the deeds of power that they had seen, saying, 'Blessed is the king who comes in the name of the Lord! Peace in heaven, and glory in the highest heaven!' Some of the Pharisees in the crowd said to him, 'Teacher, order your disciples to stop.' He answered, 'I tell you, if these were silent, the stones would shout out.'
Luke 19:28–40

If you wish, return to the reflection for Wednesday of Week 2 ('Enthroned on the praises of Israel', p. 77).

Jesus invites his disciples to enthrone him on their praises (Psalm 22:3). Jesus didn't need the praises of his followers; he was neither weak nor narcissistic and in need of 'bigging up'. Rather, God's creative and sustaining fullness overflows so that it is possible for all creation—people and stones—to be caught up in it, into a giant and joyful 'Yay!'

Prayer

May your name be held holy. Blessed is the king who comes in the name of the Lord.

Monday

The day of
Unleavened Bread

---

*Now the festival of Unleavened Bread, which is called the Passover,
was near. The chief priests and the scribes were looking for a way to
put Jesus to death, for they were afraid of the people. Then Satan
entered into Judas called Iscariot, who was one of the twelve; he
went away and conferred with the chief priests and officers of the
temple police about how he might betray him to them. They were
greatly pleased and agreed to give him money. So he consented and
began to look for an opportunity to betray him to them when no
crowd was present.*

*Then came the day of Unleavened Bread, on which the Passover
lamb had to be sacrificed. So Jesus sent Peter and John, saying, 'Go
and prepare the Passover meal for us that we may eat it.' They asked
him, 'Where do you want us to make preparations for it?' 'Listen,'
he said to them, 'when you have entered the city, a man carrying a
jar of water will meet you; follow him into the house he enters and
say to the owner of the house, "The teacher asks you, 'Where is
the guest room, where I may eat the Passover with my disciples?'"
He will show you a large room upstairs, already furnished. Make
preparations for us there.' So they went and found everything as he
had told them; and they prepared the Passover meal.*

*When the hour came, he took his place at the table, and the
apostles with him. He said to them, 'I have eagerly desired to eat
this Passover with you before I suffer; for I tell you, I will not eat
it until it is fulfilled in the kingdom of God.' Then he took a cup,
and after giving thanks he said, 'Take this and divide it among*

yourselves; for I tell you that from now on I will not drink of the fruit of the vine until the kingdom of God comes.' **Then he took a loaf of bread, and when he had given thanks, he broke it and gave it to them, saying, 'This is my body, which is given for you. Do this in remembrance of me.'** *And he did the same with the cup after supper, saying, 'This cup that is poured out for you is the new covenant in my blood. But see, the one who betrays me is with me, and his hand is on the table. For the Son of Man is going as it has been determined, but woe to that one by whom he is betrayed!' Then they began to ask one another which one of them it could be who would do this.*

Luke 22:1–23

If you wish, return to the reflection for Saturday of Week 4 ('The life of the world', p. 147).

Taking bread, giving thanks, breaking the bread and sharing it was Jesus' thing. It's what he did on the grassy hillside with the crowds and in countless homes that welcomed him. It transformed lives. What better way to remember him?

Prayer

Give us each day our daily bread; we eat it in remembrance of you.

Tuesday

Into the time of trial

He came out and went, as was his custom, to the Mount of Olives; *and the disciples followed him. When he reached the place, he said to them, 'Pray that you may not come into the time of trial.'* **Then he withdrew from them** *about a stone's throw, knelt down, and prayed, 'Father, if you are willing, remove this cup from me; yet, not my will but yours be done.' Then an angel from heaven appeared to him and gave him strength. In his anguish he prayed more earnestly, and his sweat became like great drops of blood falling down on the ground. When he got up from prayer, he came to the disciples and found them sleeping because of grief, and he said to them, 'Why are you sleeping? Get up and pray that you may not come into the time of trial.'*

While he was still speaking, suddenly a crowd came, and the one called Judas, one of the twelve, was leading them. He approached Jesus to kiss him; but Jesus said to him, 'Judas, is it with a kiss that you are betraying the Son of Man?' **When those who were around him saw what was coming, they asked, 'Lord, should we strike with the sword?' Then one of them struck the slave of the high priest and cut off his right ear. But Jesus said, 'No more of this!' And he touched his ear and healed him.** *Then Jesus said to the chief priests, the officers of the temple police, and the elders who had come for him, 'Have you come out with swords and clubs as if I were a bandit? When I was with you day after day in the temple, you did not lay hands on me. But this is your hour, and the power of darkness!'*

Luke 22:39–53

If you wish, return to the reflection for Saturday of 'Ash Wednesday to Saturday' ('In your room', p. 28).

Jesus did not go cheerfully to the cross; it was the last thing he wanted. To follow him is not to seek out suffering but to 'Get up and pray' against it. When suffering cannot be avoided, however, we are to accept it with courage and grace—and when, in our pain, we are tempted to lash out at others, to say, 'No more of this!'

Prayer

Father, do not put us to the test; yet not our will but yours be done.

The cock crows

Then they seized him and led him away, bringing him into the high priest's house. But Peter was following at a distance. When they had kindled a fire in the middle of the courtyard and sat down together, Peter sat among them. Then a servant-girl, seeing him in the firelight, stared at him and said, 'This man also was with him.' But he denied it, saying, 'Woman, I do not know him.' A little later someone else, on seeing him, said, 'You also are one of them.' But Peter said, 'Man, I am not!' Then about an hour later yet another kept insisting, 'Surely this man also was with him; for he is a Galilean.' But Peter said, 'Man, I do not know what you are talking about!' At that moment, while he was still speaking, the cock crowed. **The Lord turned and looked at Peter. Then Peter remembered the word of the Lord, how he had said to him, 'Before the cock crows today, you will deny me three times.' And he went out and wept bitterly.**

Now the men who were holding Jesus began to mock him and beat him; they also blindfolded him and kept asking him, 'Prophesy! Who is it that struck you?' They kept heaping many other insults on him. When day came, the assembly of the elders of the people, both chief priests and scribes, gathered together, and they brought him to their council. They said, 'If you are the Messiah, tell us.' He replied, 'If I tell you, you will not believe; and if I question you, you will not answer. **But from now on the Son of Man will be seated at the right hand of the power of God.'** *All of them asked, 'Are you, then, the Son of God?' He said to them,*

'You say that I am.' Then they said, 'What further testimony do we need? We have heard it ourselves from his own lips!'
LUKE 22:54–71

If you wish, return to the reflections for Tuesday of Week 5 ('Because he first loved us', p. 160) and Friday of Week 3 ('The hope to which he has called you', p. 114).

As Jesus is questioned, he makes it clear that his reign is imminent: the kingdom is now. Previously in the courtyard Jesus has looked at Peter. He remembers Jesus' words and he weeps in remorse, an indication both that forgiveness is needed and that the relationship itself has not been destroyed. This becomes evident when Peter and Jesus are reunited over bread and fish (John 21): first comes the fellowship meal of reconciliation, and only then comes the hard talk about Peter's discipleship.

Prayer

Your kingdom come; and forgive us our sins.

Handed over

Then the assembly rose as a body and brought Jesus before Pilate. They began to accuse him, saying, 'We found this man perverting our nation, forbidding us to pay taxes to the emperor, and saying that he himself is the Messiah, a king.' Then Pilate asked him, 'Are you the king of the Jews?' He answered, 'You say so.' Then Pilate said to the chief priests and the crowds, 'I find no basis for an accusation against this man.' But they were insistent and said, 'He stirs up the people by teaching throughout all Judea, from Galilee where he began even to this place.'

When Pilate heard this, he asked whether the man was a Galilean. And when he learned that he was under Herod's jurisdiction, he sent him off to Herod, who was himself in Jerusalem at that time. When Herod saw Jesus, he was very glad, for he had been wanting to see him for a long time, because he had heard about him and was hoping to see him perform some sign. He questioned him at some length, but Jesus gave him no answer. The chief priests and the scribes stood by, vehemently accusing him. Even Herod with his soldiers treated him with contempt and mocked him; then he put an elegant robe on him, and sent him back to Pilate. That same day Herod and Pilate became friends with each other; before this they had been enemies.

Pilate then called together the chief priests, the leaders, and the people, and said to them, 'You brought me this man as one who was perverting the people; and here I have examined him in your presence and have not found this man guilty of any of your charges against him. Neither has Herod, for he sent him back to us. Indeed, he has done nothing to deserve death. I will therefore have him flogged and release him.' Then they all shouted out together, 'Away with this fellow! Release Barabbas for us!' (This was a man who had been put in prison for an insurrection that had taken place in the city, and for murder.) Pilate, wanting to release Jesus, addressed them again; but they kept shouting, 'Crucify, crucify him!' A third time he said to them, 'Why, what evil has he done? I have found in him no ground for the sentence of death; I will therefore have him flogged and then release him.' But they kept urgently demanding with loud shouts that he should be crucified; and **their voices prevailed**. So Pilate gave his verdict that their demand should be granted. He released the man they asked for, the one who had been put in prison for insurrection and murder, and **he handed Jesus over** as they wished.

LUKE 23:1–25

If you wish, return to the reflection for Saturday of Week 1 ('Too deep for words', p. 60).

Jesus is caught in a four-pronged attack by the religious authorities, the local government, the imperial administration, and the mob. There is nothing else for him to say. Amid the hubbub of voices and actions, he descends into a silence and a stillness too deep for words.

Prayer

Jesus, when we are beyond words, let your Spirit sigh for us.

Good Friday

'Jesus, remember me when you come into your kingdom'

As they led him away, they seized a man, Simon of Cyrene, who was coming from the country, and they laid the cross on him, and made him carry it behind Jesus. A great number of the people followed him, and among them were women who were beating their breasts and wailing for him. But Jesus turned to them and said, 'Daughters of Jerusalem, do not weep for me, but weep for yourselves and for your children. For the days are surely coming when they will say, 'Blessed are the barren, and the wombs that never bore, and the breasts that never nursed.' Then they will begin to say to the mountains, 'Fall on us'; and to the hills, 'Cover us.' For if they do this when the wood is green, what will happen when it is dry?'

Two others also, who were criminals, were led away to be put to death with him. When they came to the place that is called The Skull, **they crucified Jesus there with the criminals,** *one on his right and one on his left. Then Jesus said,* **'Father,** *forgive them; for they do not know what they are doing.' And they cast lots to divide his clothing.* **And the people stood by, watching; but the leaders scoffed at him, saying, 'He saved others; let him save himself if he is the Messiah of God, his chosen one!' The soldiers also mocked him, coming up and offering him sour wine, and saying, 'If you are the King of the Jews, save yourself!'** *There was also an inscription over him, 'This is the King of the Jews.'*

One of the criminals who were hanged there kept deriding him and saying, 'Are you not the Messiah? Save yourself and

*us!' But the other rebuked him, saying, 'Do you not fear God, since you are under the same sentence of condemnation? And we indeed have been condemned justly, for we are getting what we deserve for our deeds, but this man has done nothing wrong.' Then he said, 'Jesus, remember me when you come into your kingdom.' He replied, 'Truly I tell you, today you will be with me in Paradise.' It was now about noon, and darkness came over the whole land until three in the afternoon, while the sun's light failed; and the curtain of the temple was torn in two. Then Jesus, crying with a loud voice, said, '**Father,** into your hands I commend my spirit.' Having said this, he breathed his last. When the centurion saw what had taken place, he praised God and said, '**Certainly this man was innocent.**'*

Luke 23:26–47

If you wish, return to the reflection for Monday of Week 1 ('Another garden', p. 41).

After the deed is done, the nails driven in, Jesus forgives those to whom the job has been delegated. In doing this, he shows his power over them, for they are under the authority of his Father. What he then has to bear as he hangs naked on the tree is a degree of exposure to humiliation and shaming that is one of our deepest catastrophic fears—the fear that led Adam to cover himself with skins and hide among the trees. But all that happens as Jesus is exposed and taunted is that his innocence becomes clear. There is no shame; there is no fear, because it has been cast out by perfect love.

Prayer

Father, knowing that we are forgiven, may we ourselves forgive everyone indebted to us, and one day be with Christ in Paradise.

Easter Eve

Waiting expectantly

*And when all the crowds who had gathered there for this spectacle saw what had taken place, they returned home, beating their breasts. But all his acquaintances, including the women who had followed him from Galilee, stood at a distance, watching these things. Now **there was a good and righteous man named Joseph,** who, though a member of the council, had not agreed to their plan and action. He came from the Jewish town of Arimathea, and he was waiting expectantly for the kingdom of God. This man went to Pilate and asked for the body of Jesus. Then he took it down, wrapped it in a linen cloth, and laid it in a rock-hewn tomb where no one had ever been laid. It was the day of Preparation, and the sabbath was beginning. **The women who had come with him from Galilee followed** and they saw the tomb and how his body was laid. Then they returned, and prepared spices and ointments. On the sabbath they rested according to the commandment.*

Luke 23:48–56

If you wish, return to the reflection for Monday of Week 3 ('In this place', p. 98).

The passion narratives are not all about the depths of human depravity. They also give us glimpses of the heights of human decency, of people rising to the occasion. These are signs of the stirring of the kingdom, showing what human beings can be when we 'come to ourselves'.

On this, the sixth day, we rest, we watch, we wait.

Prayer

Your kingdom come.

Remember how he told you

But on the first day of the week, at early dawn, they came to the tomb, taking the spices that they had prepared. They found the stone rolled away from the tomb, but when they went in, they did not find the body. While they were perplexed about this, suddenly two men in dazzling clothes stood beside them. The women were terrified and bowed their faces to the ground, but the men said to them, 'Why do you look for the living among the dead? He is not here, but has risen. **Remember how he told you, while he was still in Galilee, that the Son of Man must be handed over to sinners, and be crucified, and on the third day rise again.'** *Then they remembered his words, and returning from the tomb, they told all this to the eleven and to all the rest. Now it was Mary Magdalene, Joanna, Mary the mother of James, and the other women with them who told this to the apostles.*

Luke 24:1–10

If you wish, return to the reflection for Thursday of Week 3 ('Your kingdom has come', p. 110).

As we pray the Lord's Prayer, we obey the commands of the angels: we remember his words, we remember him, we remember the world, we are re-membered.

Prayer

> *Abba,*
> *May your name be held holy,*
> *Your kingdom come;*

Give us each day our daily bread,
And forgive us our sins,
For we ourselves forgive each one who is in debt to us.
And do not put us to the test.
Marana Tha

Questions for group discussion

Ash Wednesday to Saturday

- What does the example of Jesus have to tell us about the relationship between prayer and action in our lives?
- What are the various ways that members of the group have found helpful of 'getting away' and gaining a new perspective? How might we help others—especially those who have limited mobility due to ill health or age—'get away'?
- In our experience, in what ways do words help and in what ways do words hinder private prayer and public worship? What changes might we make to our practice in these areas in the light of our discussion?

Week 1

- How easy is it for group members to relate to God as 'Father'? What images pop into our minds when we think of God? Do these images relate to adults who cared for us when we were growing up?
- How might we speak about the love of God with the 'language of the heart' to folk who have no experience of a father or a bad experience of a father? What images might we explore with them?
- What is the experience (if any) of group members of the Spirit of God working in cooperation with their spirits? Are there things that get in the way of this? Are there things we can do to enable it?

Week 2

- Group members are invited to share an experience of God's 'otherness'. If this seems to be difficult, the group is invited to reflect on why this is.
- How does the idea that prayer is a job—joining in the work of Christ—affect the way we see it? How might it affect the way we experience it, especially when we don't feel like praying?
- It is perhaps easy to bless and thank God when things are going well. It might feel forced and dishonest to do this in the midst of our or others' misfortunes. How might we, with integrity, bless and thank God in the dark times?

Week 3

- What does 'looking for the kingdom' mean here and now?
- How would group members describe or explain the kingdom of God to a 'seeker' asking questions about the Christian faith?
- If the kingdom has come, how do we make sense of the suffering and injustice in the world? Does the sense we make of it have an impact on how we live?

Week 4

- How good are we at living for each day and appreciating it as a gift? How might we be better at it? What are the things to which we, as individuals and communities, need to sit more lightly?
- Group members are invited to share times when they have trusted God to meet a need. Did God provide? Was it in the way they expected?

- What might it mean for us to share the bread of life with others?

Week 5

- What is/are our 'in-group(s)' and what is/are our 'out-group(s)'?
- How can we be alongside those who find it hard to forgive and those who want forgiveness but find it hard to ask? (Include situations where the perpetrator or victim has died.)
- Can we think of occasions from our experience when church teaching has been invoked to excuse or even support abusive relationships?

Holy Week

How do the themes of the Lord's Prayer show themselves in the events of Holy Week, especially:

- Jesus' relationship with his Father?
- Forgiveness?
- The coming of the kingdom?

Further reading
on the Lord's Prayer

A. Schmemann, *Our Father* (St Vladimir's Seminary Press, 2003).

K. Stevenson, *Abba, Father: Understanding and using the Lord's Prayer* (Canterbury Press, 2000).

K. Stevenson, *The Lord's Prayer: A text in tradition* (SCM, 2004).

E. Underhill, *Abba* (Longmans, Green & Co., 1940).

Tom Wright, *The Lord and His Prayer* (SPCK, 1997).

Notes

1   J. Duff & J. Collicutt McGrath, *Meeting Jesus: Human responses to a yearning God* (SPCK, 2006), p. 7.

2   From Book 3 Chapter 56: *Quod nosmetipsos abnegare et Christum imitari debemus per crucem* ('That we ought to deny ourselves and imitate Christ by way of the cross'), trans. Leo Sherley-Price, Penguin edition.

3   *Lives of the Brethren of the Order of Preachers 1206–1259*, trans. Placid Conway OP, edited with Notes and Introduction by Bede Jarrett OP. Part IV, 'The Legend of Blessed Jordan of Saxony, Second Master General of the Order of Preachers', Chapter 31, retrieved from www.domcentral.org/trad/brethren/breth04.htm, 11 November 2011.

4   For all the other biblical quotations I have chosen the English translation that, in my opinion, best captures the meaning of the Greek or Hebrew text—usually, but not always, the New Revised Standard Version.

5   *Common Worship* Eucharistic Prayer F, based on the Eastern Rite of St Basil.

6   The transliteration used throughout this book is from the Greek form of *'Abbā* as it is found in the New Testament.

7   W. James, *The Varieties of Religious Experience* (Penguin, 1902), p. 35.

8   James, *Varieties of Religious Experience*.

9   H. Ullman & J. Wade, *Shock and Awe: Achieving rapid dominance* (National Defense University, XXV, 1996).

10 Isaiah 41:4; 43:11, 25; 44:6; 46:4; 52:6; Deuteronomy 32:39.

11 James, *Varieties of Religious Experience*.

12 Hebrews 7:25 talks of Christ 'making intercession', but the unusual Greek word used here is probably better translated

'turning' or 'meeting': M. Ramsey, *The Christian Priest Today* (SPCK, 2008), p. 14.

13 Literally 'sons of god(s)'. It is not entirely clear what this very ancient term refers to—possibly angelic beings.

14 Morning Prayer, *Common Worship*.

15 J. O'Donohue, *Benedictus: A book of blessings* (Bantam Press, 2007), p. 27.

16 D. Willard, *The Spirit of the Disciplines: Understanding how God changes lives* (Harper Collins, 1988), p. 31.

17 Discussed by Gregory of Nyssa in his *Treatise on the Lord's Prayer* (AD371).

18 But note the alternative version of 'Your kingdom come' in some manuscripts referred to earlier.

19 A. Maslow, 'A theory of human motivation' *Psychological Review* 50 (1943), pp. 370–396.

20 R. Baumeister, *Meanings of Life* (Guilford Press, 1992).

21 This use of the natural world as a source of revelation of the things of God is characteristic of Jesus of Nazareth, gave his teaching authority among ordinary folk, and shows him to be something of a 'natural theologian'. For more on Jesus and natural theology, see A. McGrath, *The Open Secret: A new vision for natural theology* (Wiley Blackwell, 2008), Chapter 6.

22 Duff & Collicutt McGrath, *Meeting Jesus*.

23 The Greek word translated 'soul' or 'self' in this story is the same word (*psuche*) that is translated 'life' in Jesus' famous pronouncement (Matthew 16:25 and parallels).

24 Literally 'happened'.

25 *Common Worship*.

26 J. Collicutt McGrath, *Jesus and the Gospel Women* (SPCK, 2009), p. 35. The story of Jesus and the Gentile woman is challenging and complex. I discuss it in much greater detail in this book.

27 For a detailed consideration, see Duff & Collicutt McGrath, *Meeting Jesus*.

28 Research into the social norms for inheritance in the ancient Near East indicates that the practice of taking such an inheritance in advance would have been unheard of and considered utterly reprehensible: K. Bailey, *Finding the Lost: Cultural keys to Luke 15* (Concordia, 1992).

29 Author unknown.

30 The NRSV translation is 'atoning sacrifice'.

31 This is probably not the same John who wrote the fourth Gospel.

32 J. Collicutt McGrath, 'Recovery from brain injury and positive rehabilitation practice' in S. Joseph and A. Linley (eds), *Trauma, Recovery and Growth: Positive psychological perspectives on post-traumatic stress* (Wiley, 2008), pp. 259–274.

Acknowledgments

*I owe a debt of gratitude to several people who,
mostly unwittingly, have helped my thinking and praying
through the Lord's Prayer: John Barton, Brendan Callaghan,
Phil Cooke, Penny Cuthbert, Bob Morgan, Nick Munday,
Rosemary Peirce, Elizabeth Thomson and Henry Wansbrough.*

ENJOYED READING THIS LENT BOOK?

Did you know BRF publishes a new Lent and Advent book each year? All our Lent and Advent books are designed with a daily printed Bible reading, comment and reflection. Some can be used in groups and contain questions which can be used in a study or reading group.

Previous Lent books have included:

The Way of the Desert, Andrew Watson
Jesus Christ—the Alpha & the Omega, Nigel G. Wright
Giving It Up, Maggi Dawn
Fasting and Feasting, Gordon Giles

If you would like to be kept in touch with information about our forthcoming Lent or Advent books, please complete the coupon below.

- -

❏ Please keep me in touch by post with forthcoming Lent or Advent books
❏ Please email me with details about forthcoming Lent or Advent books

Email address: _____

Name _____

Address_____

_____

_____

Postcode_____

Telephone_____

Signature _____

Please send this completed form to:

Freepost RRLH-JCYA-SZX
BRF, 15 The Chambers,
Vineyard, Abingdon,
OX14 3FE, United Kingdom

Tel. 01865 319700
Fax. 01865 319701
Email: enquiries@brf.org.uk

www.brf.org.uk

PROMO REF: END/LENT12

BRF is a Registered Charity